Pocket Water

Books by William G. Tapply

FICTION:
The Brady Coyne Novels

NONFICTION:
Those Hours Spent Outdoors: Reflections on Hunting and Fishing
Opening Day and Other Neuroses
Home Water Near and Far
Sportsman's Legacy
A Fly-Fishing Life
Bass Bug Fishing
Upland Days
The Elements of Mystery Fiction: Writing a Modern Whodunit

Pocket Water

Confessions of
a Restless Angler

William G. Tapply

The Lyons Press
Guilford, Connecticut
An imprint of The Globe Pequot Press

Contents

Introduction: Trying and Erring   ix
The education of a restless angler.

Acknowledgments   xv

Part I: Reading the Currents

1. Wild Trout   3
The brook is gone, but not forgotten.

2. The Master Angler of Aggravation Pool   11
*You can learn a lot about catching trout by watching a
heron.*

3. Natives   17
*Finding brook trout in Montana was like finding my
children living in some other guy's house.*

4. Tunafish Sandwiches and Other Inert Materials   23
Trout eat anything. It's all in the presentation.

5. Slingin' Streamers   31
*The rhythmic pleasures of throwing streamers from a
driftboat, and the democracy of fly fishing.*

6. The Secrets of the Littlehorn   39
It's not the Bighorn, but it's mine.

Part II: Still Waters

7. Raising Fishermen for Fun and Profit   47
*A warmwater pond teeming with life, a leaky rowboat,
a fly rod, and a child . . .*

8. Trash Fish   53
When the biggest bass of my life was a disappointment.

9. The Bass-Bug Moment 63
   A soft summer evening, a shaded, weedy shoreline . . .

10. Snakes 69
    Northern pike on the fly rod—but not if you've got a bad heart.

11. Muskies on the Limpopo 77
    A muskellunge on a fly rod? In Vermont? Well, almost . . .

Part III: Brine Time

12. Adrenaline! 89
    Screaming birds, slashing bluefish, panicky baitfish . . . and overpumped fishermen.

13. The Keeper Quest 97
    How I finally caught a keeper striper . . . by definition.

14. Mystical Tides and Peak Dawns 111
    A salt marsh is a living, breathing organism, and Fred Jennings has got it all down to a science.

Part IV: Angling for Trouble

15. Murphy Was a Fly Fisherman 123
    Murphy's Law and all of its corollaries and paradoxes derive directly from fly fishing.

16. Cautionary Tales 131
    How to lose fish.

17. It's Only a Fish 139
    Careless wading can kill you.

18. (Dis)Comfort 147
    No pain, no gain.

19. Why Knot?   155
Never trust a knot named after a person.

Part V: The Fly-Tying Fallacy

20. Simplify, Simplify   165
Woolly Buggers, anywhere, anytime . . .

21. Bill's Bow-Tie Dun (Patent Pending)   175
How to earn fame and fortune by inventing flies.

22. Fly-Tying Season   183
*How a father handed down his fly-tying wisdom—and,
eventually, his collection of materials—to a grateful son.*

Part VI. Life as a Metaphor for Fly Fishing

23. Timing   195
*Good fishing won't be good forever. Things change.
Carpe diem, baby.*

24. By the Numbers   203
*When we realized Lyle was counting our fish, Andy and I
found ourselves competing.*

25. Only Yesterday   209
*Keeping a journal intensifies the experience and keeps the
memories alive.*

26. High Stakes and Penny-Ante   217
Sometimes I find myself wishing I were somewhere else.

27. The Sweet Spot   225
I got there first. It was the other guy who had bad manners.

28. The Compleatly Neurotic Angler   233
*In which I visit a shrink who specializes in angling
neuroses.*

Introduction

Trying and Erring

If I had been born with a silver spoon in my mouth, it would have been a Johnson spoon with a strip of pork rind impaled on the hook.

More likely, it would've been a Silver Doctor.

My father, who is still well remembered as the Tap of "Tap's Tips," the column that ran monthly in *Field & Stream* for thirty-five years, was editing *Hunting and Fishing* magazine in 1940, the year I was born. He fished and hunted virtually every weekend of the year—and a good number of weeknights after he got home from the office, too—often with the era's best-known anglers, men like Lee Wulff and Ed Zern and John Alden Knight, whose articles he edited. Dad had racks of bamboo fly rods, drawers full of reels, boxes of flies, cartons of fly-tying materials, shelves of fishing books. Fishing was both his job and his passion.

Introduction

—

I was born into it, you might say. From the time I was old enough to hold a rod, Dad took me with him, and as he remembers it I caught landlocked salmon and smallmouth bass by trolling streamers in cold Maine lakes before I ever caught a panfish on a worm.

All this could easily have turned me off from fishing, and truthfully, I don't believe that those early encounters with exalted species of gamefish were what hooked me.

When I was five, my family moved to a quiet farming community west of Boston. A two-minute walk over the hill behind our house took me to The Old Res. It was a shallow, weedy, ten-acre pond fed by a trickle that dried up in the summer. A falling-down brick gatehouse at the deep end testified to the pond's origin as a reserve town water supply. The Old Res teemed with warmwater life—bullfrogs, dragonflies, ducks, herons, muskrats, leeches, turtles, snakes, and, of course, fish.

The Old Res was responsible for my enduring passion for fishing. It held no landlocked salmon or smallmouth bass, but horned pout, sunfish, yellow perch, and crappies abounded, along with the rare—and therefore prized—eel and pickerel. There were rumors that largemouths (which seemed possible) and brook trout (dubious, but who knew?) hung around secret

Introduction

springholes out in the middle, but I never caught one, and given the fact that I squandered most of my childhood on the muddy banks of The Old Res, I'm quite certain that had other species lived there, one of them would have eaten my worm at one time or another.

Still, the possibility of it made me shiver every time my bobber jiggled or the line began to snake out through the guides.

One spring evening soon after we moved to the banks of The Old Res and my fascination with it had become evident, Dad got up from the supper table, poked my shoulder, and said, "Come on. Let's get you a proper fishing pole."

This struck me as odd, since I already had my own bamboo fly rod plus access to Dad's arsenal of gear, but I followed him into the woods out back. After a lot of testing and rejecting, we cut down a poplar sapling, took it home, stripped the bark off it, and rigged it with some baitcasting line and a couple of feet of leader.

I used that pole a few times to derrick stunted panfish out of The Old Res, but it wasn't very effective. I couldn't get my bait out far enough with it, and I couldn't strip in a fish when I hooked it. After a bamboo fly rod, my pole felt heavy and stiff and unresponsive. So pretty soon I went back to using my fly rod.

I remember feeling vaguely guilty about it. For some reason, Dad had wanted me to use that homemade poplar pole.

At the time I was too young to understand, and he never did explain why he insisted I fish with a poplar sapling.

It's taken me a lifetime to understand it fully: He didn't want me to skip any steps, and given his expertise and the places he took me and all of his equipment, I easily might have.

First principles. Begin at the beginning. Learn by doing. Try and err and try again. The hard way is the best way. That's what Dad wanted for me.

I am eternally grateful.

My father was my partner, but he tried not to be my teacher. When we fished on foot, we usually went our separate ways. In boats, we took turns rowing and casting. As much as we fished together, I don't remember him ever saying, "You're doing it wrong," or "Try it this way," or "Watch how I do it." He pretty much left me alone. I imagine he had to bite his tongue many times. I learned to row by rowing, and I learned to cast by casting. That's how I learned how to find fish and get them to bite, too.

Knot tying was the one exception to Dad's hands-off approach. He insisted I learn three knots: the Turle knot (for tying a hook to a leader), the blood knot (for tying pieces of leader to each other), and the perfection loop. A fisherman could never be an independent learner if he couldn't tie his own knots.

When I fished by myself, as I did just about every day that The Old Res wasn't covered with ice, I spent a lot more time not catching fish and trying to figure out why than I did catching them. Not catching fish taught me where they didn't hang out and what they wouldn't eat and how they didn't like a bait or fly to appear in the water. Messing up a cast taught me what felt wrong. Trying it different ways led, gradually, to something that felt and worked better.

And so fishing was, for me, a continuous process of discovery. I had plenty of time to try and err. Mostly err. Failure, I learned, was the norm for fishing. Failure was frustrating, but it fascinated me, too. Every failure was a lesson. Finally getting it right, after getting it wrong for a long time, always felt like a triumph. It still does.

I've fished with experts, and although I've learned a lot from them, it's always felt vaguely like cheating. I've acquired fine equipment and traveled to some of the best waters in North America, and I appreciate them as only a boy whose father insisted he fish with a poplar pole could.

I'd still rather fish by myself. I prefer to have a guide or a local expert point me to his river and let me explore it without his help. I'd rather walk a bonefish flat alone than with a guide spotting fish for me. I don't want to be told what fly to tie on or where the fish lie or how to cast to them. That would short-circuit the angling experience for me.

I like doing it the hard way.

This consumes a lot of time that others might consider a waste. It guarantees plenty of failure. But it's the approach that gives me the most pleasure. There's nothing so satisfying as figuring it out all by myself.

If it's too easy, I get restless and go looking for something else. I want mysteries to unravel and problems to solve.

And so I continue to try and to err. I continue to mess up casts and not catch fish, and I continue to wonder why and try different things, many of which don't work, either. A day of fishing with no failure in it is a bad day of fishing. It means I haven't learned anything. It leaves me unsatisfied.

So I seek out opportunities to fail. Even familiar waters and old situations, I've found, contain little pockets of mystery if I look hard enough for them.

A lifetime of trying and erring and trying some more has convinced me that what I don't know about fishing would fill a book.

This, you might say, is that book.

Acknowledgments

Without the magazine editors who have encouraged me to muse about angling over the years, I would have no book. A long time ago Don Causey, presently the editor of *The Angling Report*, asked me to write what he called "celebrations" for the now-defunct publication he then edited and helped me shape them into essays that I could be proud of. Duncan Barnes took me into the *Field & Stream* family, where for several years my name appeared right after my father's on the masthead. Slaton White, who succeeded Duncan as editor, has been a wise mentor and a good friend. Jim Babb has made *Gray's Sporting Journal* a magazine anyone would be proud to have his name in. The editors of the Abenaki publications in Bennington, Vermont—Art Scheck, Phil Monahan, John Likakis, and Joe Healy—have generously shared their ponds and streams as well as the pages of their magazines with me. You have only to skim a copy of *American Angler*, *Fly Tyer*, *Saltwater Fly Fishing*, or *Warmwater Fly Fishing* (now, alas, no longer being published) to reaffirm the words of Sparse Grey Hackle: "Some of the best fishing is done not in water but in print."

Part I

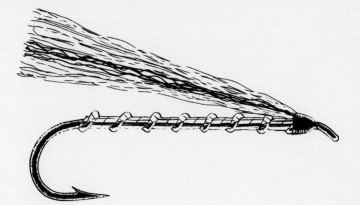

Reading the Currents

"There is no substitute for fishing sense, and if a man doesn't have it, verily, he may cast like an angel and still use his creel largely to transport sandwiches and beer."

—Robert Traver

Trout Madness (1960)

Chapter One

Wild Trout

When I was growing up, the only water we knew of in our part of eastern Massachusetts that still held native brook trout meandered through a swamp two towns away. It was too small and remote even to have a name. Its anonymity, of course, only heightened its appeal. If it had no name, I could believe that my father, who knew how to keep a secret, really had discovered it.

I could lug my rod and a can of worms over the hill out back to The Old Res anytime, and I always caught plenty of fish. But trout fishing was an Occasion precisely because it was not nearby. Trout were special because I fished for them only with Dad, and because they were scarce and hard to catch and beautiful and utterly wild.

We visited our secret little brook only two or three times a season, in April, before the larger rivers cleared up and mayflies began to hatch and we could cast dry flies. We dug worms in the morning. Dad said we needed only a dozen or so. He was right, of course, because we expected to get only a few bites, but I insisted that we gather a hundred, on the theory that you never knew when you'd hit it just right, and you certainly didn't want to run out of bait.

Our brook wound slow and inscrutable through a vast bog fed by hillside spring seeps, and we had to walk through the woods for fifteen or twenty minutes to get to it. On those early spring days we sometimes still found dirty patches of old snow in shadowy places under the evergreens. The swampy April breezes carried the faint mingled aromas of pine needles and thawing earth and skunk cabbage and rotting vegetation. The buds were just beginning to open on the alders, but the oak trees were still skeletal, and it was a dark black-and-white place hidden from the sun by the ridges and the evergreens. We often heard grouse drumming in the distance. They sounded like balky old engines trying to get started. Sometimes we flushed a migrating woodcock. We always found the tracks of raccoons, minks, muskrats, and deer in the mud.

Reading the Currents

—

5

I knew even back then that trout places could be as alluring as trout fishing.

A half-grown boy could jump across our brook in most places. Its currents were barely noticeable. It ran deep against bushes, fallen trees, and undercut banks. Its faintly tea-colored water hid its mysteries. You had to interpret its surface to figure out what lay underneath. Trout, Dad said, lurked in deep protected places. They survived because predators such as minks, herons, and kingfishers could not catch them.

Most trout, in fact, did not survive. Those that managed to were the smartest, wariest, and swiftest, and those were the ones that lived long enough to reproduce and pass along their smart, wary, and swift genes. That's why wild trout were hard to catch.

We are trout predators, Dad said. We must be smarter and warier than they are if we hoped to get one to bite.

I loved the idea of being a trout predator. It seemed to make the trout at least my equal. I liked knowing that I had to be as stealthy as a mink or a heron to catch one. I couldn't just roll-cast a worm out into the water and wait for a fish to come along and swallow it the way I did for panfish. I had to figure out where a trout might be hiding, and I had to stalk him without his knowing it. I had to drift my worm to him in such a way that he would mistake it for a natural bait and decide, despite all of his survival-tuned instincts, to pick it up in his mouth and make my line twitch.

This trout fishing did not involve sophisticated equipment or complex strategy or esoteric science. It was basic, but subtle, too. Fishing for native brook trout in this wild little brook, I understood, was a kind of hunting. It was, as worm dunking for panfish was not, *real* fishing.

Wild brook trout were *real* fish.

We hit the brook somewhere in the middle of the swamp and fished it back toward the car. I would start in and Dad would circle around the alders and willows to a spot fifty feet or so upstream from me. He'd hang his handkerchief on a bush and begin there. When I fished my way up to the handkerchief, I'd take it, circle around Dad, and hang it where I resumed fishing.

We fished as slowly and precisely and stealthily as herons. We crouched on the boggy banks and hunkered behind bushes, thrusting out our fly rods to drop the baited hooks so that they would drift deep and tight to the undercuts. It took half an hour or more to cover the distance to the handkerchief.

Thus we leapfrogged each other, always within shouting distance, always fishing virgin water. It was at once solitary and companionable.

Reading the Currents

—

As near as we could tell, no one else ever fished in our name-less trout brook. We never found footprints or cigarette butts on its boggy banks, and this, as much as the trout that lived in it, gave our brook its special romance.

The trout ran small. A seven-incher was a trophy from our brook, and we rarely killed one. We just liked to try to catch them.

They had lived there since the glaciers retreated, eons before men with spears began to hunt them. They were stained dark and coppery like the water where they lived. Their spots glittered like drops of fresh blood inside sky-blue halos, and their fins were edged with ivory. A six-incher in my hand felt cold and muscular and wild. I believed then—and I still do—that a native New England brook trout was nature's most beautiful and elusive creation. Catching one initiated the lucky boy into exalted company. It made him a mink or a heron—a hunter, a true predator, a creature of Nature himself.

* * *

Inevitably, I became addicted to fly fishing, and Dad and I began exploring big trout rivers with well-known names and reputations all over New England. But we continued to visit our brook every April. We dug a canful of worms (I continued to insist that we bring many more than we needed) and carried our fly rods through the woods to the place in the swamp that hid our secret little brook.

The day we found the surveyor's markers scattered through the swamp and along the margins of our brook was the last day we went there. When I realized what those orange stakes signified, I raced through the woods, ripped as many of them as I could find out of the ground, and heaved them into the bushes.

Dad, uncharacteristically, did not bawl me out for my blatant vandalism. As I remember it, he just stood there watching me with a bemused smile playing around his mouth.

He didn't help me rip up the stakes, either, although I believe he would have if he'd thought it would help. He knew instantly what I had instinctively realized: Progress had found our brook, and Nature, even with our help, was no match for its implacable momentum.

We fished our brook that April day, and the trout were as abundant as ever, coppery, red spotted, wiggly, and wild. We returned them all, even though we knew it was an act of quixotic futility.

Our wild trout, we knew, were doomed.

* * *

Reading the Currents

—

9

Today I live less than a mile from that brook. The forest has been cut down, the hills leveled, the swamp drained. Suburban roads intersect geometrically where our brook once meandered, and houses and garages sit where ruffed grouse used to drum in April.

Our brook now flows straight, shallow, and warm through a concrete culvert. Its muddy banks are trampled with the prints of children's sneakers. Its water is dirt-stained and carries a faint septic odor, and the only thing that glitters in it is broken glass.

Chapter Two

The Master Angler of Aggravation Pool

My local trout stream passes under a stone bridge that I cross several times daily on my way to the post office or the grocery store or the lumberyard. I am constitutionally incapable of driving across that bridge without stopping. Although I go nowhere without my car gear—patched waders, old fiberglass fly rod, spare spools of tippet, box of bedraggled trout flies, all jammed into the trunk behind the spare tire—I rarely fish in my local trout stream. It's too . . . well, local.

But I like to take its pulse, on the whimsical but compelling theory that if my little stream is doing well, all must be well with the world. So I pull to the side of the road, climb out of my car, slip on my polarized glasses, lean my elbows on the bridge rail, and study the water.

Although I don't fish in the long slow pool below the bridge, many anglers do, and I like to watch them and kibitz from the cheap seats at the bridge rail. Few trout are caught from this pool. Its lazy currents are deceptively tricky, and the hatchery trout that manage to survive their first week there have, of necessity, learned all about bait and lures and flies and two-legged giants in hip boots.

We locals call it "Aggravation Pool." It's a good place for learning lessons in angling humility, which is another reason I don't fish there. I've already earned an advanced degree in humility.

A single fisherman had taken a position in the shallow water down at the tail of Aggravation Pool when I wandered onto the bridge early one sultry evening in June. It was not the part of the pool I would have chosen to fish, but this angler apparently didn't want to wade in above his knees. He stood on skinny reedlike legs as still as a streamside shrub, and his gray-blue outfit looked, to my eyes, the same color as the sky, perfect camouflage from the point of view of a fish. He peered steadily into the water, sight-fishing, slowly working his way upstream, pausing after each cautious step—alert, poised, infinitely patient, and intensely still.

Then suddenly, and with no wasted motion, he tensed, cast, and struck.

He landed that trout quickly, then returned to his fishing.

In twenty minutes he hooked seven trout in seven casts, and he landed every one of them. It was the most impressive angling performance I'd ever witnessed at Aggravation Pool.

He kept everything he caught, which normally would have disturbed me. For those of us who live to fish and depend on a finite number of trout to provide us with sport, killing more than a couple of them for supper is self-defeating. But herons, unlike people, fish to live, and I couldn't begrudge this one the fruits of his clever angling.

Only a few decades ago, great blue herons were hunted legally in many regions, on the theory that every dead heron meant hundreds of living gamefish. It was an accurate calculation, but a seriously misguided management practice. Even today, I've heard trout guides curse the birds and make jokes about accidental roadkill with prime salmon-fly feathers and .22-caliber holes in them.

* * *

When this heron had taken his limit, he flapped away, as lumbering and ungainly in the air with his five-foot wingspread and trailing legs as he had been quick and graceful in the water. The heron is a solitary fisherman but a gregarious nester, and I figured he was headed for the rookery in the swamp over the hill, where several dozen big crude stick nests sat high in the branches of a forest of dead oaks. There he would stab his beak into the open mouths of his cackling babies, regurgitating nourishment into their throats.

A couple of evenings after watching the heron, I stopped at the bridge again. This time a human fisherman squatted on the bank fiddling with his gear. He wore a red shirt, a yellow cap, and a grim expression.

"Any luck?" I called to him.

He glanced up at me, frowned, shook his head, and mumbled something. I caught the word *aggravation*.

From the bridge rail I saw a dozen delicate rings speckling the pool's surface. "There's a few trout rising," I called to the fisherman, pointing.

He stood up, shaded his eyes, squinted at the water, then gave me a thumb's-up.

A minute later he sloshed into the middle of the stream, sending waves rolling across the water. He took a position thigh-deep in the middle of the riffle just upstream from where it dropped into the pool. He stripped line off his reel, and when he waved his fly rod, casting directly downstream, it caught and reflected the slanting rays of the sinking sun. His line threw quick shadows over the water, and the rings of rising trout disappeared from the surface.

I stood there watching, my elbows on the bridge rail, and a few minutes later I sensed rather than saw a silent shadow swoop overhead. I glanced up in time to see a heron circle the water and glide to a stop at the tail of the pool, near where I had seen him—or one of his relatives—a couple of days earlier.

I shifted my attention to this new angler. He high-stepped slowly into position, then paused, still as a stump, his neck arched like a bow at full draw, his eyes intent on the water in front of him.

A moment later his head shot forward like an arrow, then withdrew with a trout in his beak.

I felt like applauding.

The man standing in the water just below me, I noticed, had stopped casting.

The heron swallowed the fish, lifted a leg, hesitated, took one step forward, tensed, and a moment later struck again. Another trout went down his gullet.

"Hey!" The man took off his yellow cap and began waving it. "Hey, you!" he yelled. "Scram! Get outta here!"

The heron looked up, cocked his head, then bent his knees, pushed himself out of the water, and flapped away.

The man stood in the middle of the pool, shaking his head. Then he reeled in, sloshed to shore, climbed the mud bank, and joined me on the bridge.

He leaned his elbows on the rail beside me, and we gazed down at the water while the light faded from the sky. After a while, a few trout began to dimple the surface of the pool.

My companion chuckled. "I was thinking of all my tax money going down that heron's gullet," he said quietly. "But I guess I should've watched how he did it, instead of scaring him away. I probably would've learned something."

I said nothing, and the trout continued to rise in Aggravation Pool.

Chapter Three

Natives

Envy, I know, is a deadly sin, and I try to commit the deadly sins in moderation. But it's hard not to envy a man like Datus Proper to excess. Even his name turns me green.

He's written elegant and, in their way, definitive books on subjects as eclectic as trout-fly design, pheasant hunting, and the countryside of Portugal. During a distinguished career in the diplomatic corps, he fished all over the world, and during his times in D.C., he prowled the mountain streams of the Shenandoah. When he retired to Montana, he and Anna built a gorgeous home on the banks of their own little spring creek. You can watch twenty-inch rainbows sip pale morning duns off the surface while you sip gin-and-tonics from the Proper living room. If you're in the mood, you can take a rod from the garage, creep across the back lawn, and try to fool one. Datus doesn't bother his rainbows much anymore. "Once in a while I'll try to catch one," he says. "But mostly, I just like to watch them, know they're there. Having a spring creek in your backyard gives you a different attitude toward fishing."

Datus is surrounded by trout in his part of Montana, and whenever I'm out there we try to spend a day together. His little spring creek, with its super-spooky rainbows, could occupy me for a week, but ever the deferential guest, I always tell him: "Let's go someplace you'd like to go." Being a deferential guest, I've learned, is an excellent way to discover new woodcock covers and secret trout streams.

So last summer we loaded our vests, waders, and fly rods into Datus's truck, headed south, turned off the highway onto an un-marked dirt road, and soon we were winding through primeval evergreen forest and alpine meadow, climbing steadily up into the mountains. "I think you're going to love this," he said as he drove. "The Madison and the Yellowstone, places like that, they get old fast when you live out here. Too many people. Too tech-nical. They're not what trout fishing is all about."

The little mountain stream Datus took me to that day (one of the rules of being a deferential guest is never divulging the name or location of a secret woodcock cover or trout stream, so don't ask) reminded me of the stair-step brooks that rise in springs high in the Green and White Mountains and the Berkshires and the Catskills back east. He was right. I loved it instantly.

We fished Datus's creek the same way I fish those mountain brooks back home. We crept upstream, taking turns, flipping Royal Wulffs up into the quickwater at the heads of the pools, squinting at their white wings as they bobbed on the currents, alert for the quick, splashy rise of a wild little trout, and if the mountains that rose above us hadn't been snowcapped in August, if the evergreens hadn't been lodgepole pines, and if the animal that we startled drinking from the pool around the bend hadn't been a mule deer, I could've believed I was a kid again, back home, when my own mountain streams ran wild and cold and were loaded with wild little trout that splashed wantonly at attractor dry flies.

I missed several strikes before I hooked one, and when I held its cold wiggly body in my hand and saw its crimson spots with blue halos, its ivory-edged fins, and the vermiculations on its back, I looked at Datus with arched eyebrows.

"Yep," he said. "Montana brookies. Neat, huh?"

I smiled. "Natives."

* * *

Natives. That's what we called them back fifty years ago when deforestation, acid rain, pollution, highways, shopping malls, and overfishing had already made wild eastern brook trout rare and precious. Even as a boy, I'd had enough sense to treasure brookies because they were native and because I knew they were rare and precious, and I traveled far to hidden places to fish for them. They'd lived in our brooks since the glaciers receded, and except for landlocked salmon, pickerel, and a few species of panfish, they were our only native freshwater fish, and certainly the loveliest.

I liked fishing for transplanted species such as largemouth bass and brown and rainbow trout, of course. In many places, these worthy species thrived and reproduced and became "wild." But they weren't native. They'd been introduced into our waters for the purpose of catching them, and fishing for them felt vaguely artificial. It still does.

Catching hatchery-raised brook trout from streams and ponds where they once lived wild—but no longer can survive through the summer—never fails to remind me of the crimes we've committed against our land. These colorless, flabby, stupid impostors might be brook trout genetically, but they are not wild, and they're certainly not native.

Brookies still live and reproduce in a few of their native eastern waters, and there they qualify as "wild." I've caught pretty specimens from rivers like the Battenkill, little brookies that still have their parr markings. But I don't trust them. Hatchery trucks have been dumping brook trout willy-nilly into eastern waters for more than a century in their misguided effort to feed the greed of fishermen, so even those Battenkill brookies—fish that might actually carry some native DNA in their genes—doubtlessly have several shady hatchery-bred ancestors lurking in their family trees.

Truly native fish of all species are special. They've been here longer than we have, and catching one connects us to something transcendental, the way that catching non-native transplants doesn't. Yellowstone or Snake River cutthroats, Florida largemouths, and Alaskan rainbows thrill me as Bighorn browns, for example, do not.

Only a few pods of certifiable natives remain in New England. I've found them in out-of-the-way Vermont meadow streams and deep-woods Maine ponds. They bite eagerly, as is their nature, and the most appropriate way to catch them is on an old-fashioned Parmacheene Belle or Mickey Finn.

The boggy, barren muskeg of Labrador is speckled with interlinked lakes and rivers. From the air, they look like chains of glittering pearls. Lee Wulff discovered them and oversaw the construction of a few primitive fishing camps on them more than sixty years ago. Even today they're accessible only by floatplane.

Brookies to challenge Daniel Webster's legendary trout or Dr. Cook's record Nipigon River fourteen-and-a-half-pounder perhaps live in the remote, cold, shallow, nutrient-rich waters of Labrador. Ten-pounders have been taken on the fly rod in recent years. The Inuit guides don't even count anything under three pounds, and when I was there a few years ago, I caught several that weighed more than seven. They cruised the coves and slurped big brown mayflies off the surface, and the only trick was to drop a big brown dry fly in their path.

Even those giant Minipi brookies struck eagerly. Natives are like that.

* * *

Datus and I had a lovely afternoon. His gorgeous Rocky Mountain stream was full of quick, wild little crimson-spotted brookies, and they struck eagerly. I didn't have the heart to tell him that I found it vaguely disturbing. This Montana stream, I kept thinking, should have held cutthroats, its own natives, not these aliens. Brookies belong back east, where they're *our* natives, and where they are now virtually gone.

It was like finding my own children living happily in someone else's house.

Chapter Four

Tunafish Sandwiches and Other Inert Materials

High noon on the Bighorn. The August sun was blazing down from a cloudless Montana sky. The pale morning dun hatch had petered out, so Andy and I pulled our driftboat against a high bank and tossed the anchor up into the grass. I sat on the stern seat, catching some shade from an overhanging cottonwood and eating a tunafish sandwich. Andy, who considers eating a waste of precious fishing time, climbed out and began stalking a pod of sipping trout upstream from where I sat. I was admiring his stealth when a soft slurping noise made me turn to look behind me.

A good-sized rainbow trout had moved into the eddy created by the driftboat, about twenty feet downstream from where I sat.

Pocket Water

———

As I watched, his head twisted to the side and his mouth winked white. A minute or so later he did it again.

Idly I broke off a bit of tuna from my sandwich and dropped it into the water.

The trout moved into its path and sucked it in.

I fed that trout several bites of my sandwich. Each time he ate, he finned a couple of strokes upstream, moving closer to the source of this tasty new nourishment, until he hovered almost in the shadow of the boat.

Why not? I thought.

Moving very slowly lest I spook him, I picked up my rod, un-hooked the No. 18 PMD dry fly from the keeper ring, and im-paled a piece of tuna on the hook. I dropped it over the side. As it drifted toward the trout, a little surge of current caught the leader and jerked it sideways, and he turned away to let it pass. I stripped some line off my reel, shook some extra slack out through the guides, and tried again. The trout ignored it as it passed over his head.

So I dropped my tuna-PMD a bit farther upstream and guided it so that it drifted directly to the trout's nose. This time he opened his mouth and ate it.

I remained sitting in the stern as I played, netted, unhooked, and released him.

Reading the Currents

—

"Nice one," yelled Andy, who had turned to watch. "What'd he take?"

"Nothing you've got in your fly box."

I was, I admit, a bit embarrassed. Catching trout on bait—even something as exotic as a chunk of white albacore lightly dressed with mayonnaise, salt, and pepper and impaled on a No. 18 dry-fly hook tied to a fourteen-foot leader tapered to 5X—is generally thought to require luck and patience, not skill and knowledge. Most of us would rather be considered skillful than lucky. Baitfishing is for barefoot boys with cane poles and worms and more time than skill—which, presumably, is why grown-ups give up dunking bait in favor of casting flies.

And yet . . . to catch that big rainbow, I had to locate him, avoid spooking him, and present my bait so it would drift to him in a perfectly natural manner—all of which required the same skills that fly fishermen value.

"Okay," I said to Andy. "It was a short cast but a tricky presentation. He took a tunafish sandwich. And I'm proud of it. You got a problem with that?"

"Nope. I think it's kinda cool." He grinned. "You know, even with your expensive graphite fly rod and your fancy neoprene waders, you're still a barefoot boy at heart."

* * *

Pocket Water

—

Back when I *was* a barefoot boy, the only fishing outfit I owned was a hand-me-down eight-foot South Bend fly rod, a Pflueger Medalist reel, and a kinky HDH floating line. I could cast, if that's the word for it, anything with that rig—bass bugs, streamers, dry flies, spinners, miniature Jitterbugs. Mostly, though, I fished with worms. Trial and error taught me how to roll-cast so that the worm would not come unhooked, and how to lob a bobber or split shot a considerable distance.

When I fished for trout in our lazy local brooks and streams, an unweighted worm on a fly rod usually did the job. I figured out how to flip the worm up into the head of a pool and steer it through the fish-holding lies. I intuitively understood the importance of keeping my line off the water so that the worm would tumble along with the currents. I had never heard the word *drag*, but I could have explained it to you. I watched the place where my leader entered the water, and the slightest hesitation or twitch triggered my hook-setting reflex. Sometimes it meant I'd hung up on a rock or sunken log. More often, it was a trout.

In heavy currents, it made sense to clamp a split shot or two onto my leader to get it down to where I figured the fish were lurking. I wanted to feel the lead bounce and tick off the bottom. The fish I caught that way told me when I was doing it right.

Reading the Currents

—

27

* * *

Back when I was a barefoot worm fisherman, I kept most of the trout that I caught. When I cleaned them, I liked to poke through the gunk in their digestive systems. Most of it was unidentifiable, but I always found bugs in their various stages of metamorphosis—nymphs, pupae, larvae, and adults. The scientific studies I've read confirm my personal, nonscientific conclusions. Aquatic insects make up about 95 percent of most trout's diets. The remaining 5 percent is comprised of small fish, crustaceans, and what the scientists call "other inert materials," stuff like pebbles and twigs and cigarette filters.

I don't recall ever finding an earthworm in the belly of a trout I caught on a worm, nor do the scientists report that earthworms are a significant part of trout menus.

And yet the history of fishing proves that trout eat worms whenever they come tumbling along—not to mention San Juan Worms (which apparently imitate something that most trout have never before eaten), Glo Bugs (which anglers like to believe "imitate" salmon eggs, but which I've found effective in waters where no salmon live, and in midsummer, when no fish of any description are spawning), and inert materials such as feathers and fur arranged on fishhooks to resemble—at least to the angler's eye—mayfly or stonefly nymphs.

* * *

Why do trout eat earthworms—and twigs, pebbles, Glo Bugs, and tunafish sandwiches? Why, for that matter, do they eat our clever imitations of subsurface aquatic insects? In the case of worms and tuna, perhaps it's because they smell edible—although in neither case can the odor be familiar to the fish.

Glo Bugs, San Juan Worms, and nymphs, we like to believe, look like actual trout food. When we catch trout on these lures, we congratulate ourselves on successfully "fooling" them by imitating what they like to eat.

When trout are feeding selectively, as they sometimes do (though probably less often than we think), it may help to imitate what they're eating. Most of the time, though, I believe any barefoot boy who can drift a worm—or even some inert material such as a Glo Bug or San Juan Worm—onto a trout's nose without drag will catch it. Trout use their mouths the way we use our hands—to feel and test and explore their world. They are always hungry and curious, and they'll bite down on anything that looks remotely edible.

I'm positive that Bighorn rainbow had never eaten canned albacore tuna before I shared my sandwich with him. But he was curious. So he tried it, he liked it, and he looked for more. Still, when I impaled a piece of tuna on a hook, he refused to eat it until I managed a perfectly drag-free drift.

I suspect I could have caught him on a nymph, Glo Bug, San Juan Worm, or some other inert material, too. But I'm rather pleased that I persuaded him to eat a piece of my sandwich. It reminds me that I haven't forgotten what I learned as a barefoot boy.

Chapter Five

Slingin' Streamers

We picked the first week in October to return to the Bow River. Peter Chenier, our old guide, had assured us that early autumn on the Bow was a great secret—Indian summer in Alberta. Low, clear water, high puffy clouds, hoppers all day, big, aggressive prespawn brown trout that gobbled blue-winged olives whenever there was overcast. Warm days, cool nights, crowds pretty much gone.

Peter called every day during the week before we left. His reports were always the same: plenty of bugs, rising trout, shirtsleeve weather, gorgeous foliage.

Well, Andy and I didn't usually worry about weather. But this time we'd finally persuaded Randy Paulsen to join us for his first fly-fishing excursion. He'd been listening to our stories long enough, he agreed. He was ready to try it. For Randy's sake, we hoped the weather would hold.

We advised him on gear, and he'd bought the best. We told him to get some casting lessons, and he promised he would.

We were winging our way westward to Calgary when Randy mentioned that his weekend of lessons had been canceled. "Don't you guys worry about it," he said. "I'll manage. I tried a few casts on my lawn and got it out there okay. Anyway, I know I'm gonna have fun."

Our plane circled the runway in Calgary for an hour. It was midnight when we finally touched down. A blizzard had come sweeping across the Alberta plains.

In our hotel room, when Randy went into the bathroom, I turned on the TV. The weather channel forecast more snow, temperatures around zero, big winds from the west—forty gusting to seventy. "It's not as bad as it sounds," said Andy. "That's centigrade or something."

"Bad enough," I mumbled. "Anyway, I was thinking of Randy."

"Oh, he grew up in Utah. He understands snow."

"Yeah, well, I was thinking of me, too."

Andy grinned. "So we'll be slingin' streamers. What's wrong with that?"

"Absolutely nothing," I said. "Except one of these days I'd like to throw streamers voluntarily, not just because the weather's lousy and no trout are rising and it's the only way to catch 'em."

"We could do that."

"Yeah," I said, "but we never do."

After sharing driftboats for close to twenty years, in fact, Andy and I have developed into what we modestly consider a deadly streamer-slingin' tandem. Each of us has evolved his own variation on the standard Woolly Bugger. Andy calls his "The Fly That Ate Montana." Mine is the "Mongrel Bugger." We generally prefer black and purple for river trout on dark days or in discolored water, but we go with shades of orange, yellow, and brown for autumn brown trout. We rig them on 7- or 8-weight rods, sink-tip lines, and stubby leaders, and we cast them tight to the fallen logs, current seams, foam lines, sweepers, boulders, and eddies along the riverbanks. The guide tries to slow the driftboat's downriver progress and hold us fifty feet from the bank.

Andy and I quickly find a rhythm. From the bow, he throws at a forty-five-degree downstream angle. A quick upstream mend to keep his fly in the trout's zone for an extra couple of seconds, a few hard strips, lift, locate another target, cast. No false casts, no wasted motion. From my station in the stern, I watch Andy with one eye, and while I'm retrieving one cast I'm picking my target for the next.

We figure we each make an average of two casts a minute. If each cast averages fifty feet, this calculates to more than two miles of fly line that we sling in an hour, barring interruptions from fish, snags, sandwiches, or pauses to knock ice from our guides, blow feeling into our fingers, and watch eagles circle overhead. Some days we sling streamers for ten straight hours.

Some days we don't catch many fish. But when we do, they're usually big ones.

On our earlier trip to the Bow, in fact, several arm-length brown trout had engulfed our streamers. They made swirls the size of washtubs. Our memory banks were stuffed. We were eager for more of it.

* * *

At seven o'clock the next morning, the riverbank was white, the sky sooty. Hard kernels of snow blasted directly upriver, almost horizontal. Three Massachusetts anglers and two Canadian guides stomped their boots on the frozen riverbank and slurped black coffee. "Day before yesterday," said Peter, "half a dozen twenty-inch browns were lined up along that bank right over there." He pointed. "Crashing hoppers, eh?"

"No more hoppers this year," said Andy.

"No," said Peter. "But the trout aren't going anywhere."

We agreed that Bob Lowe should guide Randy, the rookie. Peter would row Andy and me. We would take what Peter called "the scenic route"—if you're into grain elevators, skyscrapers, and bridge abutments. The downtown stretch of river, he said, was where spawning brown trout tended to congregate in the fall. Sounded good to us.

We pounded the banks hard for two hours. We had a few bumps, swirls, tugs, and follows. They were hitting short. We hooked no fish.

In the middle of the morning we drifted past Randy. He grinned and held up two gloved fingers. A V for victory? A question: Any luck?

We shook our heads. No, we hadn't caught anything, either.

He yelled, waving his V sign in the air. Over the rush of the river, we heard him yell, "Two. I got two."

Andy and I pumped our fists. I held up my hands, palms facing each other. How big?

He showed us. Fifteen or sixteen inches.

Well, good. It's important that the rookie catch a fish or two.

A little farther on, Peter held the boat beside an eddy under a highway bridge. "Throw it in there," he said, jerking his chin at what was clearly the steaming outflow from a sewage treatment plant. The snow-swept wind carried a faint sulphur odor. A slimy green weed grew along the current seam. Trucks rumbled overhead. "Hotspot, eh?" grunted Peter.

Then we were both hooked up. Doubles, twin eighteen-inchers. I caught another. Andy lost one. Okay. This was more like it, even if it wasn't exactly a wilderness experience.

It was the middle of the afternoon by the time we caught up with Randy and Bob. Andy and I had each landed another trout.

Randy told us matter-of-factly that he'd caught two more since we'd seen him. How big? One was twenty-one, said Bob. The other twenty-two. He'd measured them, eh?

The snow stopped the next day, but the temperature actually dropped and the wind blew harder. Andy and I pounded streamers all morning without a hit. We managed to dredge up a few smallish rainbows on nymphs in the afternoon.

Randy threw streamers all day, and caught only one fish.

That brown measured twenty-five inches.

* * *

Since that trip to the Bow several years ago, I've been struggling to extract a lesson from all this. A rank novice, a man who had never cast a fly before, who could barely, after much false-casting, flop it thirty feet from the boat, this—this *neophyte*—had landed three trophy brown trout. He had outfished two hardworking, experienced—dare I say *skilled?*—anglers on a world-class trout river.

Why?

Was it Randy's choice of fly? The speed or rhythm of his retrieve? His line's sink rate? Did he have the smarter guide?

Was there, in fact, an explanation?

Or was it just the Red Gods smiling on a very nice man? The law of averages? Poetic justice? Beginner's luck? The random democracy of the trout river?

I'm content with any one of these answers.

As much as I crave hard, scientific explanations, I also like knowing that in some things, at least, there are no answers. It's comforting to be reminded that beyond skill, experience, knowledge, and fine equipment, there will always be an X factor that preserves the mystery of trout, that reaches out to some rookie, taps him on the shoulder, and hooks him forever on fishing.

Chapter Six

The Secrets
of the Littlehorn

The Littlehorn River begins at the outlet of a small cottage-rimmed pond, follows the old Boston & Maine railroad tracks behind gas stations, strip malls, and suburban backyards, passes under three highway bridges, and ends several aimless miles later in another pond. In April, when the hatchery trucks make their deposits, the bridges swarm with fishermen who cruise red-and-white bobbers through the pools.

By June, the rocks in the riffles begin to rise above the sluggish currents. Perch and bluegills and an occasional largemouth bass move up and down from the two ponds into the pools. Except for the kids from the condominium complex, who hunt turtles and frogs there, nobody pays any attention to the Littlehorn after Memorial Day.

Except me. The Littlehorn runs less than a mile from my house. For better or for worse, the Littlehorn is my home water. I wish it offered better trout fishing. But at least it's mine, and if it were better, it probably wouldn't be my secret.

You won't find any blue line on a Massachusetts road map to represent the Littlehorn River. It's on the topographic map, but it's got a different name.

The Littlehorn is my name for it. It's got pools, riffles, and runs, exactly like Montana's Bighorn. Except it's in Massachusetts. And it's a lot smaller.

There are holes in the Littlehorn where a careless step might sent water sloshing over your hip boots. You might need more than a roll cast to reach from one bank to the other where it widens and slows below the third highway bridge. Mostly, though, it's little. Its trout are smaller and scarcer, too, and the hatches are considerably sparser and less dependable than they are on the Bighorn.

But I've caught trout from the Littlehorn in every season of the year. As far as I know, nobody else in the world can say that. But then, nobody else has spent as much time as I have probing its depths, monitoring its temperature and its insects, drifting flies through it, and just sitting on its banks watching it go by. Over the years, I've discovered where the springholes and deep under-cuts are, and I know that these are places where some of those hatchery browns go to escape April worms and July droughts. They learn to elude herons and minks, and they learn to eat insects and minnows, and gradually they become wild trout.

I know these things. So I feel I've earned the right to keep the Littlehorn a secret. I share it with nobody. If you were to ask me about the Littlehorn, I'd tell you, "Oh, they dump in some stockers in April. Good place for kids with worms. Otherwise, fageddaboudit."

* * *

One evening in mid-June a few years ago I made an exception to my rule. I was working my way upstream, floating a small white-winged Wulff through the riffles and against the banks. I was catching nothing, nor did I expect to. For now, the company of the Littlehorn was enough. I expected some March browns to come off toward dusk. I planned it so I'd arrive at the pool below the washed-out milldam at just the right time.

When I rounded the bend, I found another angler standing knee-deep in the middle of my pool. She wore baggy man-sized hip boots, a long-billed cap that flopped over her ears, a blond ponytail, and a pink T-shirt. She took turns slapping the water with her fly line and slapping the mosquitoes off her bare arms.

She was in my river, fishing in my pool.

She was about eleven years old.

I sat on a rock to watch her. She cast awkwardly and grimly. But she kept at it, apparently unaware of my presence.

Soon the sun sank behind the trees and a few brownish mayflies began drifting on the water. Upstream of the girl I saw a swirl. Then another—exactly where I knew they'd be.

I couldn't stand it. "How're they biting?" I called.

She jerked her head around. "Oh, gee, Mister. You scared me."

"Sorry."

"I never catch anything. It's fun anyway."

I got up and waded in beside her. "Let's see what you're using."

She stripped in a Mickey Finn streamer, big enough to frighten a northern pike, tied to a level thirty-pound tippet.

"Want to catch a trout?" I said.

She grinned. She wore braces. "Someday I will," she said.

"Why not tonight?"

She shrugged. "Why not?"

I told her my name. Hers was Mary Ellen. She insisted on calling me Mister. I cut off her leader and replaced it with a seven-footer tapered to 4X. Then I tied on a No. 14 March Brown. "Cast it up there," I told her, pointing with my rod tip to the place where the riffle flattened and widened at the head of the pool. "There are three hungry trout there."

She managed better with the tapered leader. On her third try the fly landed lightly, drifted barely a foot, then disappeared in a quick, silvery flash. She turned to look at me. "What was that?"

"A trout," I said. "You've got to set the hook." I showed her what I meant. She watched me, frowning.

They were nine-inch browns, survivors of the spring hatchery deposit. And they were naive and cooperative. Mary Ellen hooked the third one she rose. She derricked it onto the bank and fell upon it with both hands.

I helped her unhook it. "Want to take him home?" I said.

"Oh, no. Let's put him back."

I helped her revive her trout. When he flicked his tail and darted back into the pool, she waved and said, "Bye, bye, fish."

That was one time I didn't mind sharing the secrets of the Littlehorn.

* * *

Last July, a three-day gullywasher raised the water level of the Littlehorn nearly a foot. It was still drizzly the morning of the fourth day when I waded into the head of the pool below the first bridge.

I tied on a smallish Muddler and drifted it through the currents. I cast absentmindedly and without expectation, not even moving, just fishing that pool, happy to be there. I caught a small bass and, a little later, a hand-sized bluegill. The hum and swish of trucks and cars passing over the bridge behind me was muffled by the damp, heavy air, and as I got into the rhythms of the water, the traffic sounds subsided completely from my consciousness.

It took the big trout nearly half an hour to decide to strike. When he engulfed my Muddler, I glimpsed the golden flash of his broad flank beneath the stream's surface. He turned and bulled toward the brush-lined opposite bank, and I knew he was a heavy fish. I raised my rod tip and let the line slide through my fingers. Then he jumped, and I saw that he was bigger, by several dimensions, than any brown trout I'd ever seen in the Littlehorn. He was as big, in fact, as worthy browns I'd taken from the Bighorn.

The sounds of traffic filtered back into my consciousness, and I was suddenly aware that I was standing there, in plain sight in the middle of my secret stream, with a monster trout on the end of my line.

I considered the consequences. Then I snubbed the line around my finger and lowered my rod to give the fish a straight pull. I felt the leader tighten, stretch, then pop.

"Bye, bye, fish," I said.

Part II

Still Waters

"Reason and experience tell me that bass, particularly smallmouths, have few if any superiors among freshwater game fish. But while I am always happy if I can raise ten-inch trout to a fly, I would scorn the opportunity to fish for bass of this size. The fact that the bass fight as hard, or harder, doesn't seem to cut any ice."

—Harold F. Blaisdell
The Philosophical Fisherman (1969)

Chapter Seven

Raising Fly Fishermen for Fun and Profit

Anthropologists debate it, but I'm convinced that the hunting/fishing instinct is buried deep and solid in human DNA. This will forever frustrate the animal-rights crowd, but it's good news for the angler who dreams of a lifetime partnership in the outdoors with a kid.

Kids—boys or girls, it doesn't matter—are born with an innate love of fishing. The tug and throb at the end of a line triggers in every kid something atavistic that causes her to laugh and squeal, "I got one! I got one!" Unless some adult comes along to spoil it, that kid is hooked. If the adult nurtures it, the hook sinks in over the barb, and she's hooked for life.

Kids take naturally to the fly rod. They take naturally to fly casting, too, but it takes a while and shouldn't be rushed. A fly rod is a primitive hunting-gathering tool, a natural extension of the hand and arm. Kids like the long, limber feel of it, the way it bends when there's something pulling on the line, and the way they can maneuver a fish by swinging the rod to the side. A fly reel is the kind of straightforward mechanism kids can understand and manipulate, and it doesn't take them long to figure out how to strip in a fish without reeling.

So put a fly rod in a kid's hand. Tie on something buggy—a Woolly Worm or a soft-hackle wet fly or, even better, one of each—and take her trolling on a panfish pond. Let her hold the rod in one hand and trail the other over the side while you row or paddle—very sedately—along a shoreline. Or rig that fly rod with a bobber and a baited hook, anchor in a shaded cove, and dangle it over the side. Gradually, she will start flicking her flies or lobbing her baited hook out there by herself. That is fly casting, and if you resist the urge to tell her what she's doing wrong, she will gradually get better at it.

Kids are democratic. To them, a fish is a fish. Sunfish, horned pout, bass, trout: The main difference to a kid is that sunfish are the prettiest. All shapes, sizes, and colors of fish merit equal fas-

cination, and the more different species kids encounter, the better they like it. Catching many small fish is better than a few
large ones, although they do like the scary hard pull of an occasional big one, and they should have that experience, too.

Kids like to catch fish. Adults learn the aesthetic pleasures of
fishing without catching anything, but it's an acquired taste, and
it takes a while. So avoid trout streams, steelhead rivers, and
saltwater flats. Take your kid to a warmwater pond, slough, or
lazy creek, where life fairly bubbles in abundance and variety,
and where you're never sure what might be tugging out there at
the end of the line, but it's a sure bet that something will be.
Choose a warm, soft, sunny summer afternoon, even if you think
the fish will bite better in the rain or toward dusk, when the
mosquitoes come out. In warm waters, they bite well enough all
the time. Adults can fool themselves into enjoying discomfort,
but kids are too smart for that.

Even if you want to raise a trout-fishing partner, start her out
on panfish. Kids are big on instant gratification. They want results, and they want them now. They are correspondingly bad at
patience. They have short attention spans. Their minds wander.
They lack focus. Their entire world is a wonder. Frogs, dragonflies, painted turtles, ducks, muskrats—all those denizens of

warmwater places fascinate kids as much as fish do. They'd just as soon skip flat stones across the water as fish in it, and they love digging worms almost as much as catching fish with them.

Give them short, frequent doses of fishing. Anticipate when they'll get bored, and quit five minutes earlier. If they're not catching anything, do something else. Try frog hunting or crayfish catching. Throw stones into the water. Take off your shoes and capture some rusty beer cans from the shallows. Bring them home with you and don't make a lesson out of it. You won't need to.

Kids are, in fact, suspicious of lessons. If they don't want to bait their own hooks, if they show no interest in learning how to tie on their own flies, if they refuse to touch the bluegill they've caught and don't want to unhook him themselves, do it for them. When they're ready to try these things for themselves—and they will be, if you don't make a big deal out of it—they'll let you know. In the meantime, be assured that they're watching how you do it.

Kids are pragmatists. They don't understand the importance of artfulness for its own sake. Fancy methodology does not impress them. Results impress them. Kids want it to be simple. That's why warmwater species seduce them. They can catch bluegills, pumpkinseeds, crappies, and perch almost guaranteed, and they don't need much skill to do it. Stay out of their way. Let them learn by observing, trying, and erring, and wait for them to ask. They will become skilled, and they will ask when they're ready.

Kids love riding in boats. They like a clunky old rowboat best, especially if the oarlocks squeak and it needs to be bailed now and then. Kids can stand up in a rowboat and lean over the side to pick a water lily or just peer down into the water. They might see a big snapping turtle bottom-walking down there, and if they do, it won't frighten them.

At some point, every kid will want to try rowing so *you* can fish. For kids, rowing or paddling is fun, and the principle of taking turns comes instinctively to them. Don't tell her how to do it. She's been observing you, and she'll catch on. Meanwhile, it's your turn to fish, and you should do it. Your kid will be watching and hoping you're having fun.

Kids want to know the names of things. Notice how they grin when you say "crappie" or "pumpkinseed" or "bullhead." But beetles, aquatic weeds, wildflowers, and warblers have names, too, and to kids, they're all equally important. Kids like it when you can tell them what things are called, but they also like it when you tell them you don't know. This assures them that they can trust you.

Kids notice things that adults, intent on their angling, take for granted or have stopped noticing—the *chirr*up of red-winged blackbirds flocking in the cattails, the tick of a swallow's wingtip on the surface of a glassy pond, the arch of a heron's neck, like a fully drawn bow, just before he strikes, the pink blush of the tiny blooms on common waterweeds, the garish neon shades that dress damselflies and dragonflies, the grump and burp of a big old bullfrog. Kids marvel at the purple of a bluegill's throat and the crimson of a yellow perch's pectoral fin, and when they point it out to you, you'll marvel at it, too, the way you once did when you were a kid.

Adults can learn a lot from kids, too.

Chapter Eight

Trash Fish

One August morning several years ago, before the Montana sun had begun to burn holes in the mist, Neale Streeks rowed Andy and me across the Missouri River and beached his drift-boat downstream of a flat that bubbled and churned with more rising fish than I'd ever seen. There were, literally, hundreds of them, slashing and gulping at the Trico spinners that peppered the water.

"Oh, boy," whispered Andy as he scrambled from the boat. "Oh, boy, oh boy."

I was right behind him. "Let's be smart and orderly for once," I said. "Start at the bottom of the pod. Fish side by side. Work our way up."

"Good plan," said Andy, who had already begun to false-cast. "Oh, boy," he said again. "Look at 'em all."

"No flock shooting," called Neale, who was still in the boat fiddling with his camera. "There's some big trout in there. Pick your targets."

"What'd he say?" said Andy.

"No flock shooting," I said. "Big trout. As if we couldn't see 'em."

Usually when big browns and rainbows feed on spinners, it is with a distinct lack of ambivalence. They lie suspended just beneath the surface, lift their heads out of the water, take a mouthful or two, then drop down to chew and swallow. Persuading them to take your imitation instead of one of the thousands of naturals on the water is always a challenge. But hooking a trout that has eaten your fly is not.

So I missed the first five fish I raised out of that pod.

Beside me, Andy had begun to mumble. When I glanced at him, I saw that he had stopped casting.

"What?" I said to him. "What's the matter?"

"Whitefish," he said. "There's some trout in there. But most of them are whities."

"Which ones?"

"Ah," said Andy. "There's the rub."

Before I learned how to tell the difference between the rise-form of a whitefish and that of a trout, I squandered hours of precious Rocky Mountain vacation time stalking pods of gorging whitefish. I frittered away entire hatches trying to catch trout that turned out not to be trout. When there were no hatches, I drifted nymphs through trouty holes on waters large and small, came tight when my line twitched, felt the quick surge of a big fish, got excited . . . and landed a whitefish.

The Rocky Mountain whitefish (*Prosopium williamsoni*, if you insist) looks something like a bonefish, with the same sleek body, prominent dorsal fin, and underslung mouth. Whitefish, of course, do not fight like bonefish. They fight like waterlogged gobs of moss. They feed on aquatic insects like trout and thrive in the same waters that hold trout. But they are not beautiful like trout.

Whitefish—even big ones (and I've caught whitefish that weighed four pounds easy)—take insects off the surface with a quick, frivolous spurt of water, in dramatic contrast, once you learn the difference, to the confident, no-nonsense sip of a thick-shouldered trout. They are devilishly hard to hook, which is just as well, because when you do hook a whitefish, it's never a trout. And that is a disappointment.

Trash fish, I call them.

Bob Lamm, who guides on the Henry's Fork where they are a serious nuisance, always packs smoked whitefish fillets in his cooler. The first time I tried one, I said, "Not bad. Delicious, in fact. But it's still a trash fish."

"That depends," he said.

"On what?"

"On what you're fishing for. When I'm trying to catch a mess of whities for the smoker, I do not consider them trash fish."

"And I suppose if you were fishing for whities and happened to hang a big rainbow by accident you'd be disappointed, right?"

"Disappointed?" He shrugged. "I do not like to hang big rainbows by accident."

"So," I persisted, "in that case, you would consider your big rainbow a trash fish, huh?"

"Well," he said, "maybe I would."

Bob, of course, was yanking my chain. I knew a trash fish when I saw one, and I knew he did, too.

The Bighorn goldeneyes that take pale morning duns with a deceptively troutlike deliberation—but are as hard to hook as whitefish—are also trash fish. So are the spawning suckers that sometimes inhale weighted nymphs on my eastern streams. Ditto the yellow perch that nip like tentative trout at leech imitations twitched over weed beds.

The ten-pound gold-flanked carp that ate Andy's Woolly Bugger on the Green River one October afternoon and had us thinking *monster brown* right up to the moment he netted him—that was one of the trashiest fish I've ever met.

Oh, I've sometimes fished for them on purpose, the way Bob Lamm fishes for whitefish. I've filled buckets with perch, both white and yellow. Perch can be fun on small streamers and a 2-weight rod, and perch fillets, dipped in batter and deep-fried, make better eating than smoked whitefish. I've handlined eels off Cape Cod bridges and sight-fished for cruising carp with flies that imitated mulberries. In England, I understand, they take their chub fishing quite seriously.

When you're specifically trying to catch them, there's nothing wrong with trash fishing. But it should not be confused with sport.

And a big rainbow trout can never, by any definition under *any* circumstances, be a trash fish, any more than a whitefish is a game fish.

These distinctions all seemed clear and indisputable to me until last June.

Pocket Water

58

* * *

Lake Champlain, tucked up in the northwest corner of Vermont, is, I believe, the only place on earth where there's an open season on northern pike.

I don't mean fishing season. I mean *hunting* season.

In the spring, when big pike gravitate to the shallows to spawn, men armed with .30/06 rifles and 12-gauge shotguns wade the weed beds or crawl out on overhanging tree limbs to blast them out of the water.

It's a grand old Vermont tradition, and despite occasional grumblings from folks who worry about "sport" (not to mention safety), the state shows no serious inclination to tinker with it.

For the fisherman who'd like to hang a twenty-pound pike in the shallows on a 9-weight fly rod, the best time is during the May "hunting" season, because soon thereafter, the big ones drift back into deep water.

But none of us wanted to dodge ricocheting steel-jacketed .30-caliber bullets. So we decided to try it right after the hunting season closed. We figured there'd be at least a few gun-shy pike still hanging around the weed beds.

The first day we all could make it was a misty Friday in early June. The heavy cloud cover would make sight-fishing difficult.

Still Waters

—

The lake, still brimming with rainwater and snowmelt, was backed up in the trees. Not ideal conditions.

Saltwater streamers and sink-tip lines, we agreed, would be the best bet. Except I wanted to *see* it happen—the subtle wake that materializes and accelerates behind the fly, then the heart-stopping explosion of the attack right at the surface.

So I tied on the biggest deer-hair burbler in my box, cast it out into the weeds, and chugged it back. I moved slowly along the shoreline, probing every hole and alley in the weed beds, and for the first hour or so I fished with tense expectation.

But no wakes materialized behind my fly, and after a while my casting became rote and my attention wandered. Maybe all the pike had evacuated the shallow water . . .

Then I heard Joe yell, and when I looked I saw that his rod was bent. Five minutes later he held up a pike, a five-pounder, I guessed. Not the monster we wanted, but a worthy fish.

Art, John, Kate, and I, scattered along the shoreline, shouted our congratulations.

I began to pay attention again. Where there was one, there would likely be others.

Heaving a big wind-resistant deer-hair bug on a 9-weight rod into a misty breeze was hard work. My wrist began to ache. My casting became sloppy. I snagged a weed, couldn't pull it loose, and had to wade out over the tops of my neoprenes to free my fly. It began to rain.

I'd begun to daydream about cheeseburgers and hot chocolate when I thought I saw a bulge behind my bug. I twitched it, let it sit, gave it a sharp tug that made it gurgle, walked it back across the surface.

My imagination, I guessed.

I cast again, let it sit, gave it a jerk—and my fly disappeared in an implosion that left a hole in the water.

Yes!

I hit him, and knew I'd hooked him well. He headed for the weeds. I gave him sideways pressure, down and dirty, trying to turn him. He would not be turned. He took line, not in the racy reel-screeching manner of a bonefish or a steelhead, but slow and implacable, like—well, like a big northern pike.

"Whaddya got?" yelled Art.

"Big one," I grunted.

I managed to steer him away from the weeds. He surged at the surface, then burrowed deep. I gave him all the pressure I dared, mindful of the teeth that could saw through my thirty-pound shock tippet.

I was aware that my companions had gathered around to watch.

I didn't see the fish in the murky water until I'd steered him close enough to land.

It was not a pike.

I reached into the water, thumbed his bottom lip, and lifted up the biggest largemouth bass I'd ever seen.

I've caught five-pounders. This one was a whole dimension bigger. Seven pounds, at least. Eight, more likely. Maybe more.

"Hold it up," said Joe, who had a camera to his eye.

I did, not easily. It was a very heavy fish, a female fat with roe.

It was, in fact, the fish of a lifetime.

But . . .

But it was not a pike. It was not the fish I wanted from this lake on this day.

I've been casting deer-hair bugs against brushy shorelines and along weed beds for largemouth bass for more than forty years. On any of those occasions, I'd have been thrilled to catch this fish.

I'd rather catch a big bass than a big pike.

But this bass was an accident. A mistake. I wasn't trying to catch it. I knew I didn't deserve it.

I'd been cheated out of what should have been one of the peak moments of my fishing life.

I remembered what Bob Lamm had said about catching trout while fishing for whitefish. He didn't want to hang a big rainbow by accident. Now I understood.

I'm not quite prepared to call that Champlain largemouth a trash fish.

But I wish I could be proud of it.

Chapter Nine

The Bass-Bug Moment

I grew up casting deer-hair bugs for bass, both largemouths and smallmouths, in lakes, ponds, and rivers all over New England. It was my favorite kind of fishing—even better, I thought, than casting dry flies to rising trout, or trolling streamer flies for land-locked salmon, or fishing for any trophy that lived in the ocean.

Nothing has happened in the intervening half century to change my mind.

In every kind of fishing there is the Moment. With trout, it's when a fish tips up to sip in a dry fly. With salmon and tarpon, it's that first catapulting leap into the air. When I fished with bait, as I did obsessively as a kid, the Moment came at the first shuddering jiggle of the bobber or the first twitch of the line before it began to slither out through the guides.

Those photolike moments that signal the connection between angler and fish live forever in your memory's scrapbook, and once you've stored enough of them away, they keep you focused and happy while you're getting skunked.

With bass, the Moment comes when the flat, dark, early-evening water against a fallen tree, beside a boulder, alongside a patch of lily pads, or under an overhanging bankside bush suddenly implodes where an instant earlier a bass bug had been quietly resting.

Despite James A. Henshall's famous claim ("Inch for inch and pound for pound, the gamest fish that swims"), once you've tied into comparably sized trout or salmon—or any saltwater gamefish—you know that freshwater bass are not exceptionally swift swimmers or strong fighters or athletic leapers.

But nothing in the universe of fishing can beat the thrilling topwater strike of a big bass. It's the visible moment of connection, the moment that proves you have *fooled* him, the moment when all the predatory pugnacity of the fish exposes itself. It's a primitive, primal moment for fish and angler alike. I shiver at the memory of it. I'm sure it taps into a strand of my DNA that has survived for eons. It exposes *me* as a primitive hunter-gatherer still, a predator myself.

Fishing for bass on underwater lures and flies is—well, it's okay. Underwater techniques are surely effective, often deadly, and sometimes the only way to catch them. If catching bass were the main point of it, I would fish subsurface more often than I do. I've done plenty of it, actually—but hardly ever when the possibility of depositing the image of another topwater Moment into my memory bank was even remote.

Nowadays, when I go bass fishing, I cast floating bugs to shoreline targets. If I can't do that, I rarely go bass fishing. I've searched my soul as objectively as I can, and I'm relieved to conclude that this is not snobbishness or purism. It's just what I love to do.

My kids think I'm hopelessly old-fashioned, and I'm inclined to agree with them. I tell them I know what I like, and I admit I'm probably too old and set in my ways to change even if I wanted to. I just happen to love bass bugging with a fly rod.

Native Americans practiced a version of bass-bug fishing before Europeans invaded the continent. Lobbing out something big and buggy with a long pole and dragging it across the surface of a warmwater pond, lake or creek was an American invention, and the first way bass were caught by hook and line. So I guess I *am* old-fashioned.

It's really quite simple: I love casting deer-hair bass bugs into the shaded holes next to fallen trees on a summer's evening around that magical time when the sun has dipped behind the hills, the sky is turning purple, and a fuzzy mist is hovering over my pond, when the nighthawks, bats, and swallows are beginning to swoop and dart over the water, when its surface lies as flat and smooth as a pane of black glass, when all is silence except for the grump of a bullfrog, the creak of an oarlock, or the dip of a paddle, and the occasional spat of a bluegill, when I am alone in a canoe or a leaky rowboat, or maybe in the company of a like-minded partner who doesn't need to talk to be companionable, when my bug lands with a muffled splat, sits there long enough for the rings to widen and disappear, and then goes ploop, burble, and glug when I give it a few tugs before letting it rest some more, and when, always at the unexpected moment no matter how keen my anticipation, the silence and the water's mirrored surface—and my nerves—are shattered by the explosive *ker-SLOSH* of a big bass.

For me, this is the best way to fish for them.

Actually, the best way to fish for almost everything is on the surface where you can see it all, provided we define *best* as "most fun," and not necessarily "most efficient." I don't know many trout fishermen who wouldn't rather use dry flies. The only reason to fish for bluegills with anything but miniature topwater bass bugs is if you need to catch three bushels of them instead of only two. Pike and pickerel, which tend to lurk in bassy shallow-water places, eagerly devour big, noisy topwater bugs, and the savagery of their attack is, if anything, more heart-stopping than that of a bass. Topwater fly fishing for bluefish and striped bass and other saltwater predators produces similar results—often from fish that weigh twenty pounds or more. I've caught six-pound Labrador brook trout on deer-hair mice dragged across a current. Bombers and similar deer-hair bugs, walked across the currents, are proven Atlantic salmon killers.

Bugging with a fly rod may not be the best way to catch the most bass, or to catch the biggest bass, although I'm convinced that sometimes it is. On a few occasions I've been manipulated into trying to prove it—which I've done, at least to my own satisfaction. But *most* and *biggest* are competitive terms, and they don't interest me.

Fishing for bass with deer-hair bugs is straightforward and simple, but not simplistic. It may be less than science, but it's more than luck. Doing it right and doing it well involves practice, knowledge, and experience. Luck, of course, helps.

Bass, God bless 'em, do not behave with the absolute predictability that experts sometimes attribute to them. I'm not sure that bass have free will, and I readily acknowledge that they exhibit predictable *tendencies*. At different seasons and under different weather conditions they *tend* to gather in particular types of water, and at any given time their collective moods *tend* to cluster somewhere along a spectrum from aggressive to close-mouthed. Computers can factor all the variables and spit out reliable generalizations. Many helpful books have been written on these subjects. You can use the data to help you decide whether you want to go fishing, and if you do, where to park your boat and what to tie onto your leader.

Or you can just look out the window, sniff the air, and decide that it feels right. That's generally what I do. And even when it feels wrong, if you have the urge to spend some time on the water, that's always a good time to go fishing. Even under the least favorable conditions, you can usually find a few ornery bass that'll refuse to be predictable and that will engulf a bass bug when they're not supposed to.

It's unforgettable.

Chapter Ten

Snakes

It was a typical August morning in Labrador—gray sky, cold drizzle, windchill around freezing. In the afternoon the clouds would blow away and the sun would come out and the mayflies would hatch in the coves. Then, with luck, we'd catch a couple of those legendary six-pound Minipi brook trout on dry flies.

But for now we had to improvise. Dorman, our Inuit guide, had motored us to the foot of the lake where it narrowed, quickened, and flowed into the next lake in the chain. He held out his closed fist. "Try this," he said. He opened his hand and dropped a deer-hair mouse into mine. "Lemming," he said. "Trout eat 'em, eh?"

The trick, Dorman explained, was to heave the mouse to the opposite bank and swim it across the current on a tight line. On my third or fourth try, a wake appeared behind the mouse. I held

my breath and kept it coming. The wake accelerated—then exploded. I heaved back on my 7-weight fly rod.

My limp line sailed back over my head.

"Argh," growled Dorman. "Damn snake. Bit you off. That was
a good fly."

"Snake?" I said.

"Pike," he explained.

"Big one, huh?"

"All big ones in this lake. Damn nuisances."

"Well," I said, "let's try to catch one of those nuisances, eh?"

* * *

The Anglo-Saxons called him Luce, "waterwolf," and likened
him (in both appearance and function) to the pike, their long,
pointed weapon. His Latin name, *Esox lucius*, means "pitiless
pike." He was well named.

I had my first encounter with a northern pike when I was
about ten years old. My mother had dropped me off at a quiet
slough in northern Vermont. It was a backwater of Otter Creek,
which flowed north and emptied into Lake Champlain.
Smallmouths and largemouths both lived in that slough, and I'd
brought my father's baitcasting rod and a bucket of minnows.

It was a warm sunny day, and the bass weren't biting. But I was
content. I shucked off my sneakers and socks and sat on the

bank, dangling my feet in the water and watching my red-and-white bobber float beside a bed of lily pads. Bullfrogs grumped sleepily, and neon-colored dragonflies perched on my rod tip, and it was an altogether lazy and satisfying way for a boy to while away a daydreamy August afternoon.

I actually felt his eyes on me before I noticed him. I never saw him arrive. He just materialized. Suddenly he was hovering there absolutely motionless like a big waterlogged stick—like a pointed weapon—barely a yard from my dangling toes. He was sleek and long—as long as my ten-year-old leg, at least—and he was staring up at me out of baleful, predatory, utterly pitiless eyes.

Then, I swear, he grinned at me. His jaws slowly opened and closed, and he showed me his teeth.

After a minute, he swam over to my bobber and ate my minnow, right?

Wrong.

I didn't wait for that pike to make the first move. I scrambled away from the water and reeled in as fast as I could and got the hell away from that place. I believed then, and I still believe, that if I hadn't moved fast, I'd be walking around with about seven toes today.

I wanted nothing to do with that vicious tearing, shredding, eating machine.

Pike have fascinated me ever since.

I've caught them on live bait, and I've caught them trolling sewn bait, and I've caught a lot of them by casting swimming plugs and red-and-white Dardevle spoons into weedy bays and alongside fallen timber. There is no bad way to catch a pike.

But the best way is on a fly rod. Especially on the surface. Pike are not shy. If they'll hit a Dardevle retrieved a foot under the surface, and they usually will, they'll also crash a big deer-hair bug popped and gurgled on top.

Watching a pike ambush a floating fly is like witnessing a mugging. The strike itself is the peak moment of pike fishing and the best reason to go for them on the surface. You'll notice the wake first, a calculated, unhurried V in the water ten or more feet behind your lure. The fish keeps his distance for a moment or two, taking the measure of his target. Then, without warning, the wake accelerates. The sudden explosive attack throws spray and leaves a hole in the water.

Cardiologists advise their patients not to cast floating flies for pike.

Once hooked, pike pull hard and sometimes jump spectacularly, but they tend to submit quickly. Beware. They often allow themselves to be led docilely to the boat. Then, just as you dip your net into the water, they detonate, and if you're not ready for it, you'll find yourself holding a handful of splinters.

To incite a northern to mug your fly, use a fast but erratic retrieve and keep it coming right up to the boat. Pike often follow their prey for a long distance, attacking only when they sense that it's about to escape. So if a wake materializes behind your lure, you're more likely to trigger a strike by speeding up your retrieve than by slowing it down.

When selecting a pike floater, I follow two rules: Make it yellow, and make it noisy. The fuss and burble a flat-faced popper kicks up make it appear bigger than it actually is and will get the attention of any nearby northern. While deer-hair pike "bugs" work beautifully, they don't stand up well to those razor teeth. Foam-bodied or cork saltwater-sized poppers are more durable.

My nine-foot, 9-weight, medium-action graphite rod casts air-resistant floaters with relative ease. I use a weight-forward (bass-bug taper) floating line and a six-foot leader, with two feet of hard fifty-pound shock tippet to prevent bite-offs. Pike are not leader-shy.

I debarb my hooks and carry needle-nose pliers, which together permit easy releases and minimize encounters with those nasty teeth. Pike have bony mouths that are hard to penetrate, so I keep my hooks sharp. Even so, when a pike takes my fly, I haul back several times to drive home the point.

Pike prefer cool (around sixty-five degrees), shallow (less than fifteen feet deep) water that features cover such as fallen trees and weed beds. I like to sight-fish for them in coves and along the banks, where I can often spot them lying motionless like waterlogged hunks of driftwood, ready to ambush.

Northerns are primarily daytime feeders. Although they seem to come to the surface most readily on overcast days, I have taken plenty of pike under a bright midday sun.

During their prespawn, pike are edgy and hostile and territorial. They are early-spring spawners, and I've had good days shortly after ice-out, when every pike in the water moves into shallow water.

* * *

Dorman made a face and mumbled something about "damn snakes," but I persuaded him to take us to a cove where we could try for a big pike on a floating fly. I found a box of deer-hair bass bugs in the bottom of my tackle bag, added a shock tippet to my leader, and tied on the biggest, noisiest, yellowest bug I had.

I burbled it along the edge of some lily pads, and on my ninth or tenth cast a wake bulged the pads, eased along behind my bug, sped up, and engulfed it.

I whooped, reared back, and set the hook. The fish headed for open water. My reel screamed. "Big snake, eh?" said Dorman, and when I glanced at him I saw that he was grinning. I had converted him, I thought smugly. Even the crusty Inuit had finally seen the fun of catching pike on floating flies.

I managed to horse the big fish around to the stern where Dorman could net him. "Yes, sir," he repeated as he dipped his net. "Damn big snake, eh?"

He lifted the net from the water. It held a six-pound brook trout.

"Damn trout," I said. "Put him back, eh? I want one of them snakes."

Chapter Eleven

Muskies on the Limpopo

Gray morning clouds hung low overhead, and the water under us lay dark, still, and full of mysterious promise. The air was thick, damp, and palpable. A soft day. A fishy day. Herons stalked the shallows, flocks of ducks burst up at the approach of our boat, and a lone osprey watched the water from the bleached branch of a dead tree.

As we skimmed across the bay in Randy's boat, I spotted swirls and splashes among the reeds. I pointed, and Randy shook his head and mouthed the word *bass*. We weren't after bass today.

When we entered the river's mouth, I recalled one of my favorite children's stories, which began: "Once upon a time, on the banks of the great gray-green greasy Limpopo River, all set about with fever trees . . ." When my father used to read those words to me, they conjured up vivid images in my impressionable mind (which even then was obsessed with water), and now, more than fifty years later, I was actually seeing the river I had imagined.

In the story, a snub-nosed animal called an elephant was lured to the edge of the Limpopo River by a fast-talking crocodile. The croc persuaded the naive elephant to test the water, and when he dipped in his nose, the croc clamped down on it and tried to pull the elephant in. The elephant, of course, pulled back, and his nose stretched . . . and stretched . . . and that, children, is how the elephant got his trunk.

There was a moral to the story, of course. I could identify with that gullible elephant. I'd come to dip my nose into the Vermont equivalent of the Limpopo River.

I'd come to catch a muskellunge. On a fly rod.

* * *

Ever since I was old enough to read *Field & Stream*, I'd fantasized about muskies. They were as big and toothy and savage and sly as—well, as crocodiles. "The fish of ten thousand casts," they always called them in the stories. To me, the muskellunge was the Cape buffalo of fresh water—rare, elusive, and dangerous. The ultimate quarry, especially for the fly fisherman.

Maybe somebody somewhere was catching them on flies. But I hadn't heard about it.

When Paul Koulouris called from Vermont back in the spring, his line was as beguiling to this elephant as that of the Limpopo croc. A friend of Paul's, Randy Savage (he certainly had the right name), knew where muskies lived. Randy was a bass pro who fished every day, and sometimes he fished for—and caught—muskies. He'd once held the state record.

Randy's record had been broken a few times since. The largest Vermont muskellunge on record weighed in at twenty-nine pounds, eight ounces, and measured just six inches shy of four feet long. As far back as they were recorded, all of the biggest muskies had come from the Limpopo River. In fact, Paul told me, the only truly native muskies in all of New England lived in the Limpopo, which rose in Vermont, looped through Quebec, and then emptied into Lake Champlain.

If a muskie will eat a Dardevle or a sucker, said Paul, why wouldn't it eat a big streamer fly?

So on that soft morning in early August, I rose at three-thirty, loaded my 9-weight fly rod, my reel with matching intermediate sinking line and 250 yards of backing, and several boxes of saltwater streamers in the car, and set off for our eight o'clock rendezvous at the gas station two miles south of the border.

It was, of course, a quest that would've made Don Quixote snort milk out of his nose. Fanatics—men who lived in muskie land, Minnesota, Wisconsin, and parts of Canada, and who devoted their lives single-mindedly to fishing for them—sometimes went years between catching one, paying their dues. So I was going to spend one day casting flies in Vermont?

* * *

The Limpopo wound gray and green through the primal forest, moving with no discernible current. It was maybe a hundred feet wide, and the trees that lined its steep banks—fever trees?—arched so high that their top branches nearly met overhead. Jungly brush crowded against the edges, and fallen timber littered the water.

I had no idea what muskie water was supposed to look like. But this looked good.

We putt-putted up the serpentine waterway, wary of hidden rocks and stubs, and then Randy stopped the motor at an old milldam. A few days earlier, he said, he'd spotted a muskie there.

"One muskie?" I said.

He nodded. What did I expect, his smile said, a school of them?

This one liked to hang in the current, and Randy figured he patrolled the upper hundred yards of the river. I tied two feet of fifty-pound bite tippet to my twelve-pound leader, and Randy picked a fly from my box, a big yellow-and-green marabou Deceiver on a 3/0 saltwater hook. "Looks like a perch," he said. "These 'lunge love perch."

I took pains with my knots, retied them several times with shaky hands, imagined actually hooking a record muskie and how I'd feel if I lost it to a bad knot. I'd done things like that before.

Randy liked the rig, though he was dubious about the rod.

"I've caught some pretty big stripers and bluefish on this out-fit," I told him. "Landed tarpon over eighty pounds on it."

He arched his eyebrows. "I never caught a tarpon."

"I've never caught a muskie."

"No, sir," he said. "Not many people have."

I'd met plenty of bass pros. I knew their attitude toward fly fishing. "You think this is stupid, don't you?"

"What's stupid?"

"Trying to catch a muskie on a fly rod."

"Hell, no," he said. "I think it's cool. Why not? They're here. That fly looks good enough to eat."

I cast into the current. I cast into dark holes. I cast against the bank. I cast alongside fallen timber. I cast under overhanging trees. I don't know when it started raining, but the next thing I realized, it was coming down so hard that I could barely see my fly hit the water at the end of a cast. I kept casting. Ten thousand casts was a lot.

"You bring rain gear?" said Randy.

I shrugged. "Yes, but the hell with it. I'm already soaked." I didn't want to stop casting.

Hours passed. No muskies.

"You're not going to write about this, are you?" said Randy.

"If I catch a muskie, how can I *not* write about it?"

He smiled. "Well," he said, "I'd appreciate it if you didn't name the river."

"I know better," I said. "To me, it's the great gray-green greasy Limpopo River."

Gradually, the rain slowed to a drizzle.

"You're probably itching to throw a Dardevle or something," I said to Randy.

"Shoot," he said, "if that 'lunge won't hit that fly, he won't hit anything."

We drifted slowly down the river. I cast relentlessly, combing the holes and the fallen timber, imagining the four-foot croco-dile that might be living there. Once in a while, Randy would point to a submerged log or a dark hole and say, "I hooked one right there a few years ago," or "Friend of mine thinks he spotted one next to that boulder last summer."

"How long have you been fishing for muskies?" I asked him.

"I grew up on this river," he said. "Caught my first 'lunge when I was a teenager. He ate a foot-long sucker. I chased him up and down the bank for an hour. That got me hooked pretty solid."

"How many have you caught?"

"Actually caught?" He smiled. "Three. Hooked maybe a dozen others over the years. Got my state record in 'seventy-eight."

Randy, Paul had told me, was known throughout northwestern Vermont as the Muskie Man, the expert, the guru. He was obsessed with muskies. He was, I guessed, somewhere in his forties. He'd fished virtually every day since he was a kid, mostly right here on the Limpopo River.

He'd caught three muskies in his life.

* * *

The big streamer splatted down beside the trunk of a fallen tree. I gave it a twitch and watched the yellow-and-green shape dart and wiggle under the rain-spattered surface as the slow-sinking line took it down. I guessed I'd made close to two hundred casts by then, and hope and expectation had given way to stubborn, mindless repetition.

The shape that suddenly materialized behind my fly looked black in the gray-green water. It moved with the fly for a few feet, and when it disappeared, it showed a flash of pale yellow and left a swirl the size of a washtub on the surface.

"Hey!" I said. "Did you see that?"

"No," said Randy. "What?"

"Something behind my fly. By that tree."

"Throw it back to him, man. Quick."

My hands were shaking. Adrenaline surged. I flopped the fly back against the tree trunk. Randy was at my shoulder, looking hard.

Nothing.

"Again," said Randy.

He held the boat there for fifteen or twenty minutes. I changed flies several times. I cast and cast, tried different retrieves. The shape never reappeared.

"You think that was a muskie?" I said.

"Wish I'd seen it," said Randy. "I was daydreaming. What'd it look like?"

I told him how the dark shape had just materialized there, how it had followed my fly, and how, when it sank out of sight, it had flashed yellow in the water and left behind a swirl worthy of a crocodile.

"Could be," he said. "Yeah, maybe. The fact that he never came back, that's like a 'lunge. Give it one look, decide either to eat or not, and that's that for today. Pike or bass, they're likely to take another swipe at it."

I wished Randy had seen it, too. I might've imagined it. Wishful thinking? I was capable of that.

* * *

We kept fishing. Finally in the middle of the afternoon the rain stopped and the sun came out and the wind turned sharp. "Well," said Randy, "you wanna try for pike or bass or something? Mr. Muskie won't bite in these conditions."

"Might as well head in," I said. I had no interest in pike or bass.

"You should come back," he said. "Plan on staying a week next time."

"Don't worry," I said. "I'll be back." How many casts had I made in the eight-odd hours we'd fished? A few hundred, maybe.

I still had a long way to go to hit ten thousand, but I'd paid some dues. I was beginning to understand something about the muskie obsession.

* * *

Ten days later a clipping from Paul's local newspaper arrived in my mail. FIRE LEAVES A SCARRED RIVER, read the headline.

Dousing a fire in an animal feed supplement plant on the banks of the Limpopo just four days after I fished there, the article reported, "washed thousands of gallons of copper sulfate into the river at levels sufficient to kill fish en masse—as many as 40,000 by some estimates. . . . Fish died as the lethal brew flowed downstream."

"The fish died very fast," a Quebec wildlife expert observed. "It was like a flash flood. It was very massive."

A Vermont biologist said he'd found "a dozen species of fish—mainly white suckers—dead or stressed."

The article didn't mention whether any of the dead fish were muskies.

Randy probably knows. I'm not sure I want to.

Part III

Brine Time

"**I** like mornings best—walking a shoreline casting while searching the sea for fish. Mornings are peaceful times—those who have fished through the night are long asleep. First light brings so much hope; maybe bonito will begin to work that deep section of beach, or big bass might be finning in the first wave."

—Lou Tabory
Inshore Fly Fishing (1992)

Chapter Twelve

Adrenaline!

"There they are." Captain Andrew Cummings pointed toward the horizon. "That's what we're looking for."

From where we were drifting on the vast and empty sea, they were specks in the distance, and it took me a minute to spot them. The sky had been utterly empty just moments earlier. Now there were birds, and as I watched, more birds materialized from nowhere until there was a cloud of them hovering, darting, and diving at the water.

"Be ready," said Andrew. He gunned the motor, I picked up the 9-weight fly rod armed with a big foam popper, and we skimmed across the bay. As I watched, the flock of birds split into two parts. I heard Andrew mutter something under the whine of the motor. He aimed for the flock on the left, and as we approached, they dispersed . . . and disappeared.

When we looked to the right, that flock had disappeared, too.

Suddenly, from horizon to horizon, there was not a bird to be seen. How could a hundred gulls and terns dematerialize in a matter of minutes?

Another mystery of the sea.

Andrew cut the motor, and again we drifted.

"What were they?" I said.

"Terns mostly. A few gulls."

"I meant the fish."

He shrugged. "Blues or stripers, probably, maybe both. Sometimes you find them together. Could be albies or bonito, even. This time of year, the fish are where the bait is, and that could be anywhere. Everything's on the move, and the bay is loaded with little peanut bunker." He held up his thumb and forefinger, about the length of a peanut apart. "The fish try to corner them, pack them into tight schools, push them to the surface. When they do, it brings the birds. Out here on the bay, the fish have trouble corralling the bait. So everything moves fast. Faster than us, that time. Hard to get close enough fast enough to throw a fly at them." Then his gaze shifted and his eyes narrowed. "You better grab that spinning rod."

He gunned the motor, and we were off again, aiming for another flock of birds.

This time they waited for us, and I heaved Andrew's big homemade spinning lure under the birds. Three cranks of the reel and I was on. Then I heard Andrew grunt, and when I glanced back, I saw that his baitcasting rod was bent.

"Blues," he said. "Big ones."

They were twin fifteen-pounders, and by the time we'd pumped and reeled down and finally muscled them to the boat and released them, the birds were gone.

My fish had taken a foot-long glob of wiggly rubber material that had been molded into a crude, seductive fish shape. Andrew made these things himself. He called them "Lewinskys," perhaps because fish that should've known better couldn't resist them.

"No sense trying to imitate the bait," he said. "An inch-long fly or lure would be just one of a billion out there. You've got to get their attention. Something big like a Lewinsky or noisy like a popper. Even then, they might not notice it."

Already I was designing a fly-rod version of Andrew's Lewinsky in my head. A couple of ostrich plumes and a few strips of Flashabou lashed onto a long-shanked 3/0 hook . . .

And I was thinking how much fun it would've been to see that big bluefish crash a fly-rod popper, and how much more efficiently I could've fought him with the long rod.

But I wasn't complaining. I'll take catching fish over not catching them every day.

* * *

And so it went for most of the afternoon. We drifted and patrolled the bay, hunting for birds, and when we spotted a flock, we tried to get there before they dispersed. A few times we approached close enough to see the blues swirling and crashing under the screaming, diving birds. Sometimes we had time to get off a quick cast or two with the spinning rod before everything disappeared. Sometimes we didn't. When we did, sometimes we hooked up. Often we didn't.

The sun was low in the sky when Andrew squinted over my shoulder and said, "Okay, grab your fly rod. This could be it."

This time the cloud of birds had gathered near the shore, and even as we zoomed across the bay toward them, the flock grew.

Birds were coming from all directions, and as we closed in, I could see that the water was frothing under them. The predators had the baitfish surrounded. Andrew swung around to get up-wind, then cut the motor.

I had the big popper in the air as we drifted down on them. "Get it in the water," said Andrew. "Come on. Quick!"

The surface was churning. Bluefish humped and swirled and sometimes leapt clear out of the water. Baitfish panicked into the air like big handfuls of diamonds glittering in the low-angled sunlight. Birds screamed and dived and whirled overhead.

The big air-resistant popper fell in a heap of leader and fly line barely thirty feet from the boat.

"Come *on!*" said Andrew.

My pulse was racing. *Slow down*, I told myself. *Relax. You've done this before*.

Relax? Fat chance. We were in the middle of it—birds, bait, fish, fishermen, water, blood, salt, meat. It was a complete food chain. The air was charged with adrenaline—mine and Andrew's mingled with the furious adrenaline of the predatory bluefish, the panicky adrenaline of the cornered baitfish, the screeching adrenaline of the scavenging birds. It felt electric and primal and strangely familiar. I was part of that mix.

Another cast, also sloppy. Chug the popper. There! He had it. I heaved back, then ducked as it flew at my face.

"*Strip* strike, dammit," yelled Andrew.

"I *know* that," I muttered.

I was familiar with my stealthy, patient, predatory self. I'd waited in ambush for the torpedo shadows of giant tarpon to cruise across sand flats into casting range. I'd crept up on tailing bonefish and knelt expectantly on the decks of flats boats. I'd blown plenty of shots, but I'd hit some, too.

This was different. Now I was mindless, all boiling blood and zinging nerves, speeding on all that adrenaline, as much a participant in the savage madness all around me as the fish and the birds.

Then my brain clicked into that old predatory mode—calculating, focused, single-minded—and I felt lethal. I found my casting rhythm, that old muscle memory, double-hauled the cumbersome popper into the middle of that melee, pointed my rod tip at it, stripped hard, chugged it, made it throw water, and a bluefish hit it, knocked it into the air, hit it again, missed. I kept stripping, and then he was on.

The bluefish, the predator instantly transformed into prey, now panicky himself, surged, leapt, peeled off line and backing, sounded, ran straight at the boat, then leapt again, this time right beside us.

Andrew whistled. "Big fish."

Then my line went slack.

When I reeled in, I saw that the blue's teeth had sliced through the seventy-pound fluorocarbon bite tippet.

I sat down, suddenly exhausted, and it took me a minute to notice that the birds and the bait and the blues had all disappeared.

"Come on," said Andrew. "Rig up. Let's go find 'em again."

I shook my head. "Just being here. Being part of it. That's enough for one day. That will last me a long time."

Chapter Thirteen

The Keeper Quest

Toward dusk on an Indian summer Thursday in late September, Keith Wegener and I spotted some boils and spurting water where the outgoing tide drains the mouth of the . . . well, let's just say it was somewhere in Casco Bay. It's a good spot for stripers, and you'll have to find it for yourself.

Of course, if you'd been out there that evening, you wouldn't have seen us, because Keith and I hunt striped bass from his camouflaged L.L. Bean duck boat. Keith's boat draws about three inches, which allows us to skim over low-tide mud flats and mussel beds and prowl estuaries and beaches where conventional inshore craft don't dare go. His fifty-horse motor gets us around fast enough—and slow enough, too, when we want to throw into some rocks or comb a beach—and the boat is stable enough even in rolling seas for both of us to stand up and double-haul sink-tip lines.

Besides, it's invisible. Works quite well for duck hunting, too.

Keith gunned the motor, then cut it, and we coasted into casting range. The water was flashing with panicky baitfish, and we could see the stripers crashing and slashing at them. I dropped my olive-and-white Deceiver into the middle of that chaos, gave it a couple of hard strips, and came up solid.

I hauled back, got him on the reel, down-and-dirtied him, and a few minutes later Keith reached over the side of the boat and lifted him in. He measured the fish against the markings on the boat, then looked up at me and grinned. "Hot diggidy," he said. "You got yourself a keeper."

"You better measure him again."

He did, then nodded. "Solid inch on the safe side."

"That's my first-ever keeper, you know," I said.

"Hell's bells," said Keith, "of course I know that. You haven't stopped talking about it since I met you."

* * *

I first met the striped bass when I was a kid about fifty years ago. My father and I used to help my Uncle Woober haul his lobster pots from the tidal waters of the Piscataqua River near

Brine Time

—

Portsmouth, New Hampshire. The men steered the boat, boat-hooked the buoys, and winched up the heavy wooden traps from the bottom, and I helped cull out the shorts and rebait the traps with smelly fishheads.

When we'd finished, as a reward for our hard work, we got to troll saltwater plugs behind the stern.

I was too small to hold a trolling rod. "One of them big cows grabs ahold," Uncle Woober would say, "you'll git yourself drug into the river." I saw how hard those fish hit and how powerfully they pulled, and I believed him.

One day, I knew, I'd be big enough to hold the rod. In the meantime, it was enough just to watch how the water erupted when a big bass hit a surface plug, and how the rod bent and the reel *zizz*ed, and how Dad and Uncle Woober grunted and strained. Inevitably, the striped bass became the fish of my dreams.

I don't think it was just the way things look bigger than they really are to a little kid. I've seen photographs. Those fish *were* big. Keepers, easy, by today's standards, although there were no standards in those days. Some afternoons the men hauled six or eight three- or four-footers over the transom of Uncle Woober's lobster boat. A striper, to me, was a fish about my size.

Pocket Water

—

100

Back then, my father kept a collection of surfcasting rods in the garage, and at odd times in the summer or fall he'd lash a couple of them on top of the family sedan and head for Cuttyhunk or Nauset, Great Point or Buzzards Bay, Chappaquiddick or the Canal, places that might've been in Africa for all I knew, obviously places of romance and high adventure. Striper destinations. He'd disappear for several days with fellow striped bass fanatics Frank Woolner, Ollie Rodman, and Hal Lyman. As often as not he'd come home empty-handed, bleary-eyed, and unshaven, but sometimes there would be two or three of those boy-sized stripers in the trunk.

By the time I might've been big enough to hold my own with a thirty-pound striper, Uncle Woober had stopped lobstering and my father's surf rods were collecting dust in the garage. The stripers were gone, or virtually so, my father told me, and fishing for them was pretty much a waste of time, although Frank, Ollie, and Hal kept trying. Those men, Dad implied rather wistfully, had more time to waste than he did.

And so I grew up fishing for trout, largemouths, and, when they became common along our coast, bluefish, and more than a quarter of a century passed before I became reacquainted with the striped bass.

Brine Time

—

101

* * *

The June sun had not yet cracked the horizon. A layer of fog shrouded the masts of the moored sailboats. Art Currier steered his little runabout slowly through the harbor of the Merrimack River, heading out toward Plum Island where, we'd heard, the blues had showed up. We wanted to catch some on the fly rod.

My 9-weight was rigged with a big white Deceiver and eight inches of wire shock tippet. I stood up in the bow, watching the water, but it was Art who saw the birds first, a screaming mob of terns and gulls wheeling and diving in the fog.

My line was already in the air as we drifted into casting range. Panicky baitfish were silvering at the surface, sometimes leaping all the way out of water, and beneath them I could see the flashes and boils of slashing predatory fish.

My fly landed a little short. I began stripping—and it stopped, almost instantly. I reared back, driving home the hook. From behind me I heard Art grunt. I turned my head. His rod was bent, too.

"I dunno," he muttered. "Doesn't feel like a blue."

It wasn't. A few minutes later, each of us landed a striped bass. They were twins, a shade under twenty inches long. Miniatures of those fish of my dreams.

We released them hastily, cast toward the school, and hooked up again.

By the time we landed those fish, the birds had followed the tide a hundred yards downriver. While Art fired up the engine, I clipped off my wire tippet and tied on a popper. A few minutes later Art and I were doubled up again.

We chased that school of stripers for more than an hour before we lost them. We figured we'd landed more than a dozen fish apiece, and every one of them was an inch either side of twenty.

We fished hard for the rest of the morning and never had a strike. No surprise there. Stripers were an anomaly. We'd heard they were on their way back, but that was the first evidence we'd seen of it.

That happened fourteen years ago, and although I'd grown up in New England and had squandered most of my life on the water, until that morning on the Merrimack I'd never caught a striped bass.

* * *

Since then I've caught hundreds, and I'm not alone. Casting flies for stripers has become the fastest-growing sport on the East Coast. Saltwater veterans are putting away their surfcasting outfits and taking up the fly rod. Trout anglers are investing in 10-weight outfits. Deep-sea guides have stowed their bluewater charts, trolling rods, and loran to explore inshore waters. Everyone is discovering that stripers eat flies and pull hard.

Thanks to some nick-of-time restrictions on both sport and commercial fishing, Northeast striped bass populations have rebounded from near extinction. Now schools of linesides swarm our beaches, rocks, jetties, estuaries, and tidal rivers from April through October.

The new regulations gave me what was, admittedly, an arbitrary goal: I wanted to catch a keeper on a fly. A keeper, I believed, defined a big striper, a striper to rival those my father and Uncle Woober used to catch when I was too small to catch them myself. A keeper striper was the fish of my dreams.

Under the first Massachusetts regs, any striper under thirty-six inches had to be returned. In those years I landed several that measured between thirty-two and thirty-four. When they reduced the definition of a big bass to thirty-four inches, I couldn't seem to land one much over thirty, and when they dropped it down to thirty, the best I could do was a few twenty-eight-inchers.

After a while, I came to believe that I'd been cursed.

It seemed that all the saltwater fly rodders I knew spoke matter-of-factly of the keepers they'd taken. "You just gotta be in the right place at the right time with the right fly." They'd shrug.

I was grateful for their wisdom. Very instructive.

My quest for a keeper became an obsession. I just wanted to land one. I didn't plan to actually keep it.

I was happy to catch stripers, whatever size they were running. I did not sneer at schoolies. But that keeper, that boy-sized Big One that had haunted me since I was a kid on Uncle Woober's lobster boat, continued to elude me.

Inevitably, I fell in love with the variety of challenges and puzzles that fly rodding for stripers presents. They suck in hatching cinderworms like trout taking mayfly emergers. They cruise beaches, mussel beds, and mud and sand flats, making "nervous water" and sometimes tailing like bonefish. They look like tarpon ghosting under the surface, and they'll suck in little sand eel imitations if you can drop one in their path. I've caught them on top with poppers and from deep holes with fast-sink lines and lead-eyed Clousers. I've caught them from tiny tidal creeks on trout-sized streamers and from breaking surf on hand-sized Deceivers. I've caught them at all times of day and night, from boats and from shore, in wind and rain and blistering sun, from early spring to late fall.

Sometimes they strike anything you throw at them. Sometimes they completely ignore you.

If you want to figure out how to catch striped bass on a fly rod, says Lou Tabory in his excellent book *Inshore Fly Fishing*, there's no substitute for "time on the water." He's right, of course. The only problem is that learning an ocean would take more time than I have left.

Even learning a tiny piece of it is a full-time job. The fact is, regardless of how abundant stripers are, you can't cast randomly into the ocean and expect to catch any. There are plenty of right places, but there are an infinitely greater number of wrong ones.

The right places, moreover, are constantly changing. Stripers are always on the move, and figuring out where and when you can intercept them requires factoring in a mind-numbing array of variables: time of day or night, phase of moon, tide, wind, season, weather, depth, structure, water temperature, and the availability and movement of bait. I know I've forgotten some of them.

Even when you get it all right, you've still got to be lucky. Striper fishing is endlessly complicated, more challenging, compelling, and mystifying than even trout fishing. It's hard not become obsessed with stripers.

Because the combinations of variables shift continually, what you figured out yesterday won't necessarily help you today, as Phil Craig and I discovered one night on Martha's Vineyard. We'd done our homework, and at sunset we were stationed on the jetty by the bridge where a strong ebbing tide was washing bait out of the pond. It was, according to all the locals—many of whom were there with us—the current hotspot, the place to hang a keeper on a fly.

We cast into the darkness until the tide turned without a strike.

"We slaughtered 'em at Lobsterville," we kept hearing the next day. "On that wind, you gotta be over on that side of the island."

Oh.

* * *

"I can show you some keepers," Rip Cunningham told me a few Junes ago. "Catching one is another matter. Meet me at four."

"You probably mean A.M.," I said.

"You want a keeper?"

"I'll be there," I said.

We caught stripers from rips, channels, and underwater structure. Nice fish, many of them, but no keepers. At one point, Rip climbed onto his platform and poled me across a sand flat, and we saw several big ghosty shadows. Keepers, I guessed. But the sun had just cracked the horizon, and by the time we spotted the fish in the glare, they were already scooting.

We were working a channel edge with Clousers when I hooked one that felt bigger by another dimension than any striper I'd ever hooked. It took me into my backing, turned, and raced back past the stern.

When Rip glimpsed it, he whistled. "Big fish," he whispered.

A minute later my line went limp. I reeled in and saw what I dreaded and expected: a pigtail at the end of my leader instead of a fly.

"Bad knot," I observed redundantly.

"Too bad," said Rip. "That was definitely your keeper."

* * *

Time on the water. Too much water, not enough time.

So I've learned to poach off what other men have learned from their time on the water. I've followed tide and bait and rumor from the Connecticut River to the Kennebec, either in the company of certifiable striper pros like Andrew Cummings, Tony Biski, Nat Moody, Cooper Gilkes, and Fred Jennings, or with amateur obsessives like Phil Craig and Rip Cunningham. We've found stripers crashing pogies in the rips, sucking molting lobsters off the bottom, gobbling sand eels on mud flats, and corralling herring and silversides in little tidal creeks.

I've had some marvelous fishing. But until last September, I'd never landed a keeper.

* * *

After we double-checked the accuracy of his measurement, Keith got dreamy-eyed. "Let's see . . . baked, I think, with Ritz cracker crumbs, lemon wedges, fresh-ground pepper. Boiled new potatoes, greens from the garden, that bottle of wine I've been saving—"

"Wait a minute," I said. "That's my fish. Put him back."

"Huh?" Keith rolled his eyes. "It's a keeper, man. Keepers are to keep."

"I've always vowed I'd put back my first keeper."

He grinned and held up the fish. "Look at it," he said.

I had to smile. Twenty-one inches of striped bass—a legitimate keeper, according to Maine's very sensible new twenty- to twenty-six-inch slot limit.

"Release him," I said, "and I promise I'll catch us another one."

"This is the first keeper you've ever caught in your long and futile life, and you think you're going to do it again?"

"Hey," I said. "I'm an old hand at it now."

In fact, that school was full of Maine keepers, and each of us landed and killed one in short order.

It was almost dark when something else grabbed my fly, and when I set the hook I knew it was no mere twenty-one-incher. Images of my father hauling those thirty- and forty-pounders into Uncle Woober's lobster boat flashed in my head.

I worked the big fish alongside Keith's duck boat, close enough for both of us to get a good look at him, before the hook pulled out.

I slumped on the seat and mumbled something about still being cursed.

When I looked up, Keith was laughing.

"What's so damn funny?" I said.

"I don't know what you're so upset about," he said. "That was no keeper. That fish was way too big."

Chapter Fourteen

Mystical Tides and Peak Dawns

Fred Jennings is shortish and roundish, and he wears Coke-bottle glasses, a bushy red beard, and baggy Bermuda shorts. He looks like some kind of academic—an economist, maybe, with a Ph.D. from someplace like Stanford, a guy whose idea of fun is collecting variables and compiling data and crunching numbers and creating charts and graphs, a man who might coin a term like *expected fishing quality index* and refer to it as *EFQI*.

He doesn't strike you as a striped bass guide or a mystic.

In fact, Fred Jennings is all of these things.

He guides anglers who he believes share his appreciation for the magical beauty of a salt marsh at dawn. He charges varying fees, depending on, um, the EFQI of the day.

I've fished for stripers with all kinds of experts under just about every conceivable condition. I've fished wrecks and rocks, rips and surf, mussel beds and sand flats, tidal ponds and tidal creeks. I've fished from lobster boats and flats boats, duck boats and sailboats, float tubes and waders. I've fished at midnight and midday and every time in between.

Until I met Fred Jennings, I thought I'd done it all.

"We've got a peak tide on Monday," he told me on the phone, and I could hear the edgy enthusiasm in his voice. "You gotta join me."

"What," I said, "is a peak tide?"

That's when he started to sound like a number cruncher, and I had to interrupt him. "Maybe you should just tell me what time to be there," I said.

"No later than three-thirty," he said cheerfully. "That's A.M., as in the morning."

"On second thought," I said, "I guess you better tell me what this 'peak tide' thing is."

It sounded complicated when Fred explained it, a calculus that factored in, among other things, tide, moon phase, month, and sunrise. What it amounted to, I finally understood, was that he wanted to leave his dock on the little salt creek three hours after the high tide. We'd drift with the stripers as they followed the outgoing and intercept them at the estuary where they congregated at dead low. When the tide turned, we'd move with the fish back up the creek.

You can follow this schedule anytime, of course, Fred told me. But the best time—what he calls the "magic morning"—is when the optimal tide for departure—full plus three hours—occurs at first light, ninety minutes before sunrise.

"It's downright magical on the marsh that time of day," Fred said reverently. "No boats, no motors, no people at all except maybe a few clammers. We'll see egrets and ospreys. The water's flat and quiet then. No wind. Maybe a little mist blanketing the water, the hollow gong of a bell buoy off in the distance, the squawk of gulls. We'll spot stripers cruising the shallows, sticking their tails out of the water to eat shrimp and crabs off the bottom, or boiling and crashing after baitfish. They're on the feed that time of day, and after an undisturbed night, they're usually not skittish. We'll be casting to stripers the whole time. Oh, you'll love it out there on a peak dawn."

Fred has lived on the edge of the salt marsh all his life. He's tuned into its rhythms. He knows its pulse, how it empties and fills twice every day, and he knows how baitfish follow the breathing of the tides, and how stripers follow baitfish. Between May and October, he told me, there are just twelve peak dawns, those magic mornings when all the variables line up perfectly.

I could hardly pass it up.

"Bring your trout rod," he said before we hung up. "No need for heavy gear. We'll be making short casts in shallow water. No need for waders, either. We won't get in deep, and the water in the marsh is about twenty degrees warmer than it is outside. Oh, did I mention? We travel by canoe. We drift down on the out-going, and back on the incoming. That way, we merge with the marsh's natural rhythms."

More mysticism from the economist.

Fred's even written a desktop-published book about it. It's a quirky mixture of a statistician's fact, a naturalist's theory, a fish-erman's conviction, and a romantic's infatuation. What bubbles through it all is his love for his marsh at first light, when a dip-ping paddle makes the only sound and the exhaling tide leaves sand islands and mussel beds dry—and striped bass leave wakes in ankle-deep water.

It was still dark when Fred and I lugged our gear over the long boardwalk that spanned the tidal marsh from his backyard to his dock on the creek. We rigged up our 5-weights, slipped his canoe into the water, and began to drift on the ebbing creek toward the estuary.

Fred waxes perfectly evangelical about trout-weight rods and unweighted flies and barbless hooks for schoolie stripers. "Mostly," he says, "we're catching and releasing eighteen- to twenty-four-inch fish. A 4- or 5-weight rod with an eight-pound tippet is just right. A light rod sort of goes along with the canoe. We're not throwing sink-tip lines in the wind, because we fish shallow water at first light, before the wind comes up. If there's too much wind, we just stay home. I've caught some keepers this way. Landed a thirty-eight-incher last summer on my 2-weight, as a matter of fact. That was a kick."

We beached the canoe at places where Fred's experience had taught him we'd find pods of fish, places with names like Gravelly Island, The Candy Store, The Goodie Bar, and Orgy Flat, his private names that you won't find on any nautical charts. And it was exactly as he had promised: soft, mystical, bountiful.

We caught no big fish, although we saw some. But we caught twenty-inchers more or less continuously, and they pulled awfully hard on our trout rods. Best of all, we were there to see the colors of sunrise bleed into the sky over the salt marsh.

Once, as we were drifting down on the quiet tidal currents, I spotted a tail poking up near the shore. "There," I whispered, pointing.

"Looks like a nice fish," murmured Fred. "Let's go get him."

The fish continued to work the shallows as we slid past him in the canoe. We beached it on the sand a hundred yards downriver. "Go easy," whispered Fred. "They can be spookier than bonefish in this skinny water."

I crept cautiously along the sand bank, now exposed by the half-gone tide, lurking well back from the water's edge. As I got closer, I went into a crouch, and I finished my stalk on hands and knees.

I was thirty feet back from the water when I started my line in the air. A couple of quick sidearm false casts, keeping the line well away from the fish's cone of vision . . .

And that's when I heard the motor.

I glanced downriver, and against the pink-and-pewter first-light sky I saw the silhouette of a dory chugging up the creek toward us.

"Clammer," hissed Fred from behind me. "Damn."

The little boat with the outboard hadn't even reached the place where we'd beached the canoe, at least three hundred feet away, when my striper panicked. That's when I realized that I had been stalking not a single, but a school of fish. The thin water I'd been sneaking up on exploded, and a dozen frenzied stripers burst out of there.

"Well," said Fred, "that shows you the difference between a canoe and a motorboat. We slipped past those fish, no more than twenty yards from them, and they never noticed. But that motor spooked 'em from a hundred. Too bad. Those were big fish."

We caught stripers every place we stopped on the outgoing tide. We caught them from the estuary on the ebb, and we caught them on the incoming tide as we followed it back to Fred's dock on the creek. It was tempting to believe that it didn't matter where we fished, that the stripers were everywhere, and that anybody who could throw a fly beyond his rod tip would nail them.

When I suggested this to Fred, he grinned. "Not hardly," he said. "I've spent my life learning these holes and currents, places where bait congregate and stripers ambush them. And I can't get lazy, because the hotspots keep changing. That's what makes this fishing addictive. Everything's always moving and changing. The creek's never the same."

Fred fishes fast, all eager exploratory impatience. He marches along the water's edge, casting, retrieving, mimicking the creek and the fish, always on the move. "If I don't get a hit, I keep going," he says. "There's a lot of fish here, and a lot of holes where they hang out. But there's a helluva lot more empty places, and stripers don't stay still. They're constantly following the bait and the tide. To catch 'em, you've gotta do the same."

We caught a lot of stripers. Fred caught most of them. He's a modest man, and like many skilled anglers, he prefers to deflect credit to his fly. He showed me a nondescript bucktail. "I call it the Captain's Special. The only fly I use. It seems to imitate about all the bait they eat. As the season progresses and the bait grows up, I just tie on bigger and bigger Captain's Specials."

The truth is that Fred Jennings has a nose for stripers. It's really rather mystical.

Fred's little creek lies on the Massachusetts North Shore, somewhere between Boston and the New Hampshire border. He makes those who fish with him swear not to divulge its location. "There are dozens and dozens of tidal creeks around here," he explains, "and mine is really no better than any of the others. The entire North Shore is one big estuary, and there are dozens like it up and down the entire Northeast coast. I'm positive my methods would work equally well anywhere. All these creeks are full of stripers, and they all breathe in and out twice a day. But mine is—well, it's mine, and the last thing I want is for it to be invaded by motorboats and guys with big clunky tackle. I want to reserve this little creek for canoes and light fly rods and my friends and a few compatible clients. I don't mind sharing my methods. In fact, I want to promote them. But I'd just as soon not share my creek. So," he says, fixing me with hard stare, "don't tell."

I won't.

Part IV

Angling for Trouble

"It takes several years of serious fishing before a man learns enough to go through a whole season with an unblemished record of physical and spiritual anguish."

—Ed Zern

Are Fishermen People? (1951)

Chapter Fifteen

Murphy Was a Fly Fisherman

Over the years, mystery has swirled around the identity of the genius who discovered Murphy's Law. Some say he was the engineer responsible for the safety devices on the *Hindenberg*. For a while, it was widely believed that Murphy had worked as a high-level political operative for Richard Nixon in 1972 and was the very man who coined the acronym CREEP (Committee to Re-Elect the President).

Many people assume that Murphy was a Boston Red Sox fan.

Others claim that Murphy's Law was not propounded by Murphy at all, but by somebody else with the same name.

There are even people who, stunned by the brilliance of the Law, assume that Murphy never existed. These skeptics argue that no man could single-handedly discover the one universal principle that governs all human endeavors and natural events. Any law that eluded Aristotle, Newton, and Einstein would surely escape someone named Murphy.

These are all myths. Murphy existed. I fished with him.

* * *

I met Murphy many years ago in Dillon, Montana, where he was a barber who sold beer and Woolly Buggers out of his shop and guided eastern fly fishermen on weekends.

Murphy never said, "If anything can go wrong, it will."

What he actually said was: "You shoulda been here last week"—which, of course, amounts to the same thing.

Murphy also said, "You can't get there from here. But if you could, it wouldn't be anyplace you'd actually want to go to."

His now-famous Law, along with its sundry corollaries, theorems, axioms, and codicils, all derive from Murphy's common-sense observations on fly fishing.

One evening he was telling me about a beaver pond he had found. It took half a day, he said, to hike to it, over mountains and through woods and swamp. If the rattlers didn't get you, the mosquitoes would eat you alive, and the brown bears would scavenge your leftovers. But the pond was loaded with giant cutthroats, and I wanted him to take me there.

Murphy refused. "The more unknown the place," he said solemnly, "and the longer and more arduous the trek, the more likely someone will already be there ahead of you."

I pondered this for a moment. Then, grasping Murphy's wisdom, I said: "By that logic, our best chance for privacy is to go someplace nearby and well known."

Murphy rolled his eyes. "It don't work that way," he said. "Somebody will be there, too."

Murphy and I traveled all over Montana in his mud-caked old pickup. After one particularly long drive down a potholed dirt road that seemed to be leading nowhere, I asked him if we were lost.

"Lost?" he said. "Listen. If you don't care where you are, you can't be lost."

"And everybody's got to be somewhere," I said.

"Exactly," he said. "No matter where you are, by golly, there you are."

It was Murphy who taught me that the man who snores the loudest is always the first one to fall asleep in a small cabin.

He used to say: "You'll never need your toenails until you cut them off."

One July morning when I was loading my gear into Murphy's truck, he pointed at my landing net and said, "Leave that damn thing here."

"Why?"

"Obvious," he said. "If you bring a net, you won't need it."

"And if we don't bring a net," I said, "we'll wish we did, right?"

"Not necessarily," he said.

After one particularly miserable day on a river with Murphy, I said, "I think I'm catching on. When you forget your foul-weather gear, it always rains." When he started to speak, I held up my hand. "But if you bring it, it'll rain anyway, right?"

He grinned and nodded.

"And if you tie up a dozen elegant Pale Morning Dun emerger patterns the night before," I continued, "the bugs won't hatch the next day—unless you forget to bring them with you."

"Don't try to make 'em hatch by forgetting your flies," he advised. "That don't work."

"Okay," I said. "How's this? If you don't keep checking your tippet for nicks and scrapes, you're bound to bust off the biggest trout of the season. But if you do check it, you'll never hook a fish."

"Now you're catchin' on," he said.

Although many of Murphy's Truths have erroneously been attributed to sages in other fields—mathematicians, philosophers, diplomats, theologians, auto mechanics, supermarket checkout clerks, the Grateful Dead—the fact is that Murphy discovered them, and they all originated with fly fishing.

He died last year, which reminded me of Murphy's Second Law ("If you want to be famous, you gotta die"), its First Corollary ("Everybody dies"), its corresponding Paradox ("Hardly anyone is famous"), and the Perverse of the Paradox ("If you do become famous, it'll be for the wrong reason").

Murphy would've disowned me if I'd divulged his identity or shared his wisdom while he was still alive. But now that he's gone, I don't think he'd mind. As he used to say, "Maybe it ain't over till it's over, but when it *is* over, it's for-damn-sure over."

Here, then, are some of the immutable fly-fishing truths that my old friend Murphy shared with me over the years:

- When you bust an expensive graphite fly rod, the warranty expired last week.
- If you drop a reel onto the pavement, it's your new Abel, not that old Pflueger Medalist.
- If there's one loose screw in the bottom of the drift boat, it won't catch your line until you hook a big fish.
- If there's only one bush behind you, it will move to snag your backcast.

- You should always spit on a fly for luck . . . but if you spit on a dry fly, it will sink.

- The longer it takes you to stalk a rising fish, and the more times you have to change flies and lengthen your tippet and shift your position to achieve a drag-free drift, the greater the likelihood that it's a whitefish. (Murphy's Rationalization: There's nothing wrong with whitefish; and the corresponding Fallacy: The hell there ain't.)

- When all the trout are rising on the other side of the river, the water is always an inch higher than the top of your waders. And:

- Wading halfway across is always easier than wading back. But:

- If you can wade across a river comfortably, there's never a reason to.

- If you're fishing alone and succumb to the temptation to dip your Glo Bug in store-bought scent or try the San Juan shuffle, someone will be watching. Later this came to be known as the Rockefeller Principle: "Never do anything you wouldn't want to be caught dead doing."

- The Converse of the Rockefeller Principle: You always catch your biggest trout when you're fishing alone on a catch-and-release stream without a camera.

- Just tie on a Parachute Adams. This axiom has been generalized to read: "A good solution can be applied to any problem."
- When a day of fishing begins well, it'll end badly; when it begins badly, it'll get worse.
- If a rising trout looks easy to catch, it'll be difficult; if it looks difficult, it'll be impossible.
- When you expect to do well, you'll get skunked; when you expect to get skunked, you will.
- When you misplace your forceps, you'll find them in the last place you look . . . unless you look there first.
- It takes longer to tie a fly than to lose it.

* * *

The last time I talked to Murphy on the phone, I asked him how the fishing was. "Lousy," he grumbled. "Which means it'll get worse."

"Why are you always such a damn pessimist?" I said.

He laughed. "Because it's impossible for an optimist to be pleasantly surprised."

Chapter Sixteen

Cautionary Tales

Andy and I had floated the Box Canyon with superguide Bob Lamm several times. Bob had heroically waded the turbulent, boulder-strewn river bottom, holding the stern and walking the driftboat down so that Andy and I could dredge the channels with weighted stonefly nymphs and probe the seams and eddies around the rocks with black Woolly Buggers, and we always caught lots of trout. On almost every trip, in fact, we'd taken one or two nineteen- or twenty-inchers. They were fat, strong, and beautiful, fish to be proud of.

But we'd never managed to hook into one of those legendary eight- or ten-pound Box Canyon rainbows that Charlie Brooks wrote about, and Bob had always seemed vaguely apologetic when we drifted out of the canyon. He insisted that those monster trout still lived there. Andy and I weren't so sure. Many years had passed since Brooks fished the Box.

One August afternoon after the PMDs had quit hatching on the Railroad Ranch, Andy and I decided to hike down into the canyon and kill a few hours before the evening hatch. Wading those heavy currents was a good way to drown but a poor way to cover the water, and our expectations were not high. But it was shaded and solitary and pretty down there . . . and there *were* those rainbows of legend.

Andy began working upstream, lobbing nymphs, while I decided to fish downstream. I selected a black Bugger that I'd tied on a fine-wire jig hook designed for crappies. The shape of the hook and the hunk of lead behind the eye sank it quickly, gave it an enticing action, and tipped it upside down, reducing snags.

I quickly got into the hypnotic rhythm of it, throwing that heavy fly at a slight upstream angle, mending quickly, steering and jigging it along the seams and through the channels, two careful steps downstream, throw it again, the river thundering in my ears . . . and when my Bugger stopped halfway through a drift, I figured I'd hooked a boulder.

Then the boulder jumped.

Maybe that rainbow was only a twenty-four- or twenty-five-incher. But at the time, and still, in my memory, he measured at least thirty inches. He hung over the water long enough for me to take a permanent mental snapshot of him. He looked as long as some steelhead I've measured, only fatter.

Then he was gone.

I reeled in, sat on a rock, and shakily lit a cigarette.

Some time later—it might've been a few minutes or an hour—Andy sat beside me. "You okay?" he said.

I nodded. "Sure. Fine."

"Thought I heard you yell. Worried you might've fallen in."

"Nope. Had a fish on for a minute."

"Any size?"

I looked at him. "It was an omigod Big One."

He squinted at me. "Man," he said, "you're trembling all over. What happened?"

I shrugged and showed him my black Bugger. The hook was bent open. "He got away."

Andy nodded. "Yeah, they usually do."

* * *

The Big One That Got Away is, of course, the cliché that we anglers (not to mention our skeptical nonangling friends) most cherish. It got to be a cliché because it contains wisdom and truth.

Let me count the ways:

After three days of hard hunting and futile casting around the Turneffe Island archipelago off the coast of Belize, I finally hooked my first permit. As far as I'm concerned, any permit qualifies as a Big One. But this one happened to be *big*.

On his first run, he took out 150 yards of backing in about five seconds. I hung on, cranked back line when I could, let him run when he insisted, and after twenty minutes he silvered beside the boat.

"He's beat, mon," whispered Taku, my guide. "You got heem."

At which point my rod went limp. I reeled in and found the telltale pigtail on the end of my leader. I showed it to Taku.

"Bad knot," he said. "No excuse, mon."

"Wrong," I said. "A bad knot *is* an excuse. You've got to have an excuse."

I've always particularly hated that bad-knot story, but Andy is partial to his own. After a long day of muscling heavy Clousers into the teeth of a thirty-knot October wind along the Cape Cod beaches and catching occasional schoolies, he finally sank his hook into a Big One. Andy's striper did not run as fast as my permit had. On the other hand, it was probably twice as big. He couldn't turn it, and he couldn't chase it. He held his rod high while the fish headed for the Chesapeake Bay . . . and then his reel stopped turning.

But his line kept going.

We stood there watching the entire length of his fly line head south while Andy reeled in his backing. Bad knot.

I couldn't begin to count the number of big trout that I've broken off at a wind knot (our happy euphemism for what happens when we throw a tailing loop) that I knew was there but was too lazy to repair.

I've ticked rocks on my backcast or retrieve, then lost fish because the hook point, which I hadn't bothered to check, was bent or broken.

When mayflies are popping and trout are gobbling, who can blame us for tying hasty clinch knots, for failing to lubricate them and tighten them and test them and trim them carefully?

I lost the biggest bonefish I ever hooked when the handle fell off my reel in the middle of his second run.

Hooks with rusty eyes will fray leader tippets. Unlubricated reels will catch and grind when big fish are running against the drag. I've popped several tippets that way.

The biggest fish I've ever hooked on a fly rod was a Belize tarpon that leapt seven times beside the boat. He was almost as long as I am tall. Ninety pounds was Pancho's estimate, and Pancho has seen hundreds of tarpon. It happened to be the first tarpon I'd ever hooked, and when he started to take line, I did the only thing I knew how to do: I held on. I kept holding on when he stopped way out there to roll at the surface, and I held on some more while he swam around regaining his strength, dragging my entire line and half of my backing around behind him until, inevitably, he came unbuttoned.

"You gotta be aggressive with Meester Tarpon, mon," said Pancho afterward. "Show heem who's boss. Bring heem in queek. Hook just wore a hole in his mouth. That's what happens, you not aggressive. Down and dirty, mon. You gotta fight heem hard, you know?"

Well, the truth was, I *didn't* know. I'd read all about tarpon fishing. Everything, that is, except what to do once you'd actually hooked one, which strikes even me as a poor excuse.

* * *

Big Ones have taught me a lot of lessons. They are hard lessons, and the cliché has it right: The fish I most remember are those that got away. So why do I still find myself using light-wire crappie hooks for alligator rainbows, tying careless knots, failing to test and repair my equipment, and not knowing what to do if I actually hook a Big One?

The fact is, I have a negative attitude. I always go fishing *hoping* to catch a Big One, but I never really *expect* it. Call it superstition, but all the fussy preparations—testing for and repairing the weak links in my equipment, planning and practicing what to do if I hook the fish of a lifetime—strike me as a good way to guarantee that I will never encounter that fish.

Half a century of fly fishing has taught me this: The best way to hook a Big One is to be genuinely surprised and unprepared when it actually happens.

And I didn't even mention the king salmon that ate my purple Woolly Bugger in Alaska's River Tal and decided to swim all the way back to the Cook Inlet. . . .

Chapter Seventeen

It's Only a Fish

On October 14, 1983, Ken Miyata drowned while fishing the Bighorn River in Montana. He was alone, and nobody knows exactly what happened. But it's pretty clear that Miyata had some kind of wading accident. In the fall, when they double or triple the volume of water released from the Yellowtail Dam, the Bighorn becomes a big, brawling river. Its bottom is cobbled with slick, mossy rocks. There are heavy rapids, deep holes, and sudden drop-offs.

I didn't know Ken, but I know many fishermen who did. They all say he was an experienced, enthusiastic, and skilled angler who knew his way around trout rivers.

It's useless to speculate on what might've happened that day. But the fact is, Ken Miyata lost his life while fly fishing for trout.

Wading fishermen drown in rivers every year. It's rarely obvious exactly what happened. Their bodies are usually recovered a
few miles downstream a day or two later.

Wading accidents don't always take place on big treacherous
rivers like the Bighorn. Smooth currents and shallow riffles
can flow with deceptive force and disguise ice-slick bottoms.
Heedless, headlong wading even in calf-deep water can produce
a fall that will, at minimum, drench you and ruin your day. You
can crack your head or break your wrist in a foot of water.

Or worse.

My fishing partner, Andy Gill, is a tall, strong guy, and an
aggressive wader. He takes chances I won't take, and it fright-
ens me when he does. I tell him he has a "depth wish." He's a
psychiatrist, and he laughs at my pun. But I don't mean it as a
joke.

I'm a cautious wader. Even so, I've taken my share of tumbles
in rivers. So far, I've been lucky. Once I soaked my camera beyond repair. Another time I sprained my thumb so badly that I
couldn't grip my rod for a week. Usually my biggest complaint is
that I've ruined a pack of smokes.

I'm actually grateful for an occasional drenching. I think of
each accident as an object lesson. It reminds me of Ken Miyata

and what could happen. When I'm wading a trout river, I try not to press my luck, and I wish my friends wouldn't, either. I'm quite content to cast to the fish I can reach without risking my life.

It doesn't matter how young, strong, and athletic you are, either. Make a mistake and the river can get you. Ken Miyata was just thirty-two when he died.

Andy is the kind of guy who believes that the trout on the other side of the river are always bigger, or more abundant, or hungrier. When he tells me he's going to wade over and check them out, I say, "Hey, listen, man. They're only fish."

He grins and does it anyway. So far, he's always made it.

* * *

If you wade-fish in rivers, some accessories will increase your safety and comfort:

- Rubber-soled boots provide no traction on slippery stream bottoms. Felt soles are better. For the most secure footing, wear cleats.
- Polarized sunglasses allow you to see the bottom through the surface glare and avoid a disastrous misstep.

- A wading staff gives you the stability of a "third leg" so you can pick your way over slick streambeds and through powerful currents. I know some macho anglers who sneer at wading staffs. I tell them that fly fishing isn't supposed to be a test of anybody's manhood.

- An emergency flotation device (EFD) could save your life by keeping your head above water should you find yourself careening downriver. Some wader suspenders and fishing vests come equipped with a CO_2 cartridge and a rip cord you can yank if you take a tumble.

- A belt snugged around the waist of your waders will prevent them from instantly filling with water if you step in over the top or take a spill.

- Thermal long johns under your waders will help keep your legs warm. Wading boots should fit loose enough to allow good blood circulation to your feet under two pairs of warm socks. For coldwater wading, wear neoprene waders. Numb legs and feet make you awkward and increase your chances of losing your balance, stumbling, and falling.

* * *

Intelligent streamcraft is as important as the right equipment. Here are some tricks to help you stay alive when wading:

- If water and air temperatures are warm, try wet wading. Without the bulk and weight of waders, you'll be more surefooted both in and out of the water. Wear good wading boots and shorts or quick-drying pants.

- When standing in strong currents, keep one foot planted upstream of the other. If you face directly up- or downstream with both feet perpendicular to the flow, it takes only a slight stumble, a momentary loss of balance, or a sudden surge of current for the river to knock you over.

- When you're ready to move into a new position, take a moment to study the river. Plan a diagonal route that will enable you move with one hip against the current.

- If you need to follow a fish you have hooked, don't chase him through the currents. Head for shore and play him from calm, shallow water or, better, dry land.

- Don't try to cast and wade at the same time. When you're moving in a river, give your full attention to it. If you can see the bottom, study it before you move your feet. If you can't see it, go slowly and feel for your next secure step before shifting your weight onto your forward foot.

- Don't try to step—and never jump—from rock to rock, whether they are above or under the surface. It's safer to wade on the river bottom than on boulders.

- Wade behind large rocks, where the currents are cushioned, rather than in front of them, but beware of the deep holes that often form there.

- Never fish treacherous waters without a partner nearby. Keep an eye on each other. Don't challenge each other to take risks.

- Don't wade unfamiliar streams—or a familiar river that flows fast or has even a mildly treacherous bottom—at night. Even if you don't intend to try any risky wading, never fish alone after dark.

- Whenever you want to cross swift currents, link elbows with your partner and do it together. Four feet on the bottom is several times more secure than two.

- When fishing dam-controlled waters, get to shore at the first sign of rising water. In some tailwaters, the release of water can come suddenly and without warning.

- Always respect the power of moving water. Even the most benign-looking, smooth-flowing rivers can carry surprising force.

- If you find yourself shivering, get out of the water fast. Hypothermia can sneak up on you, causing poor judgment and and numb, unsteady legs.

* * *

Above all, always follow this simple wading rule of thumb: When in doubt, *don't try it*. The potential reward—no matter how big that fish might be—is never worth the risk. After all, it *is* only a fish.

Chapter Eighteen

(Dis)Comfort

Phil and I were sitting on the back bumpers of our cars breaking down our rods after an afternoon of so-so fishing on the Deerfield. He held up a bottle of water. "Want some?"

"Thanks. I'm parched." I took a long swig. "Thirsty work, fly fishing under a blazing August sun."

"That," said Phil, "is a well-known fact."

I swatted away a mosquito that was boring a hole into the back of my neck.

"Need some insect repellent?" said Phil. "I've got some Ben's here."

"It's a little late for that," I said. "They about ate me alive on the river."

"You didn't carry repellent with you?"

I shrugged.

"What about sunblock?"

"Didn't think of it." I began to shuck off my waders.

He cocked his head. "You always wear blue jeans under your neoprenes?"

"If I happen to be wearing jeans that day."

"Isn't that uncomfortable?"

I touched my pants. They were, of course, saturated with a hot afternoon's worth of my sweat, as were my socks and my boxers.

Phil was peeling off the thin, skintight long johns he'd been wearing under his waders. I pointed at them. "Maybe," I said, "I should get me some panty hose."

"What is it with you old-timers?" he said. Phil is a whole generation younger than me, and he won't let me forget it. "Do you *like* being uncomfortable?"

"A little discomfort is good for you, sonny," I said.

* * *

The fact is, I've never gone out of my way to be miserable. On the other hand, I don't shy away from it, either. It has always seemed to me that a little discomfort adds some spice to a day of fishing.

Angling for Trouble

—

My mother used to roll her eyes at me and say, "Don't you know enough to come in out of the rain?"

Well, no. Or the snow, or the blazing sun, or clouds of black-flies or mosquitoes, either. Not when there are fish to be caught. Many of my fondest angling memories are associated with discomfort bordering on misery. To put it another way: If I hadn't suffered, I might not remember those times at all.

* * *

A pretty June evening on Grand Lake Stream. Perky hendrickson duns were drifting down the river, and landlocked salmon were taking them with quick, spurting rises.

Vicki, who had lived in Maine and knew about blackflies, had brought a headnet for the occasion. She waded downstream, aiming for a couple of fish she'd spotted feeding beside a boulder toward the tail of the pool. I plowed upstream through the heavy currents to get within casting range of a lineup of risers against the opposite bank.

When I got into position, I looked back. Vicki had disappeared: probably found some new fish to work on around the bend.

I had a thought: *I hope she's all right.* The thought, I'm ashamed to admit, passed quickly. That sort of thing happens to me when I'm looking at rising fish.

The salmon weren't hard to catch, and in the couple of hours before dark I landed six or eight of them and missed several others. They ran to a size—sixteen to eighteen inches, not big for landlocks—and after a few athletic leaps, they came quickly to my net.

I found Vicki back in the car, reading a paperback novel under the dome light.

"How'd you do?" I said.

"I did good. Read four chapters."

"I meant the fish."

"I didn't fish," she said. "I lasted about two minutes." She cocked her head, squinted at me, touched my face, then showed me her finger. It was wet with blood. "What's *wrong* with you, anyway?"

"Wrong?" I said. "I caught about half a dozen nice salmon on dry flies. I am excellent."

"The blackflies ate you alive. You're a mess. Your face is all swollen and bloody. Looks like a glob of hamburger! I told you you should've worn a headnet. I bet you didn't even use repellent. What're you, some kind of masochist?"

I shrugged. "Blackflies don't particularly bother me."

That night I alternated between fever and chills. I vomited several times.

That was a memorable evening of fishing.

* * *

I've floated western rivers so many times that they tend to merge in my memory—the rivers, the trout, the scenery, the company . . . except for the sunny August afternoon ten years ago when Neale Streeks rowed Andy Gill and me down the Missouri. That was the day that Andy foul-hooked a muskrat on a No. 10 Whitlock Hopper. Andy played the animal deftly on his 3X tippet, and in the heat of battle, we didn't notice that the wind had shifted and the temperature had plummeted and black clouds had darkened the sky. By the time Neale netted, revived, and released Andy's muskrat, hailstones the size of cherries were bouncing off our heads and accumulating in the bottom of the driftboat.

Andy and Neale quickly pulled on their hooded foul-weather gear.

I, of course, had forgotten to bring mine. So I huddled there in my T-shirt shivering uncontrollably while the hail turned to pelting rain. After a while, the rain softened, and a shaft of sunshine cut through the clouds. A rainbow appeared over the mountains and touched the ground on both ends.

Then, just to get my blood circulating, I tied on a big orange-and-brown bucktail and began throwing it against the bank. Big cannibal brown trout chased it for the rest of the afternoon.

That night, as I lay in my motel bed wrapped in blankets and sneezing and blowing my nose, Andy said, "That was dumb, forgetting your rain gear. You probably got pneumonia."

"We had good fishing, didn't we? Bet you never caught a muskrat before."

"It would've been just as good if you hadn't been miserable."

"No pain, no gain," I mumbled between chattering teeth, and I think I believed it.

* * *

I spent one January morning standing waist-deep in the estuary of a Maine tidal river trying to catch a sea-run brown trout. Never had a strike, but I'll always remember how the seawater around my neoprenes was considerably warmer than the onshore wind, which cut right through the old wool coat I was wearing. When it came time to wade to shore, my partner had to drag me. My whole body had gone numb.

The same thing happened when I got caught in a lake-effect blizzard on New York's Salmon River. Didn't get a strike that day, either.

One sweltering summer morning I walked about two miles across a dusty field to a remote section of the Henry's Fork. I was wearing my vest and my neoprenes, and when I finally got to the river, I shucked off my waders and sat down in the water. I don't remember whether I ended up catching any fish, but I do remember how good that frigid water felt on my overheated body.

On another broiling Rocky Mountain summer's day, I fainted from dehydration in the middle of an intense yellow sally hatch on the Bighorn. Keeled over in the water (which, fortunately, was only calf-deep). I had actually remembered to bring a bottle of water with me. But how can a man think about drinking when the river is boiling with big brown trout?

* * *

My friends don't believe me, but I am neither a masochist nor a stoic. I don't regard suffering as manly, and I don't seek it out. Usually the discomforts associated with fly fishing are minor and tolerable—a little heat, a little cold, a little rain, a few biting insects, hunger, thirst, sunburn. Sometimes they're more extreme, and when I'm unprepared for them, I suffer—which, by definition, is unpleasant.

Discomfort is relative to expectation. I began fishing long before the invention of Gore-Tex and Polartec and other space-age fabrics. Waders were made of canvas or rubber. They weighed a ton and always leaked, and when my feet and legs got soaked, I never knew whether it was a new leak or just my own sweat.

Usually it was both. So whenever I wore waders, I was uncomfortable. You get used to it.

Rain gear was just as bad. Wearing a canvas or rubber slicker was like being locked in a sauna. Getting rained on was refreshing by comparison.

In those days, before the invention of deet and sunblock, no so-called repellent actually repelled blackflies, and only shade kept off the sun. So I got bitten and sunburned and kept fishing, because the only alternative was not to fish.

Over the years, I've learned some lessons about comfort. My problem is, comfort isn't something I've ever associated with fishing, and minor discomfort doesn't bother me. So when I plan for a day of fishing, I still focus my attention on my tools—flies, rods, leaders—rather than on accessories designed for my physical comfort.

* * *

A couple of weeks after Phil and I fished the Deerfield, I received a parcel in the mail. It contained a pair of thin, skintight long johns. The pamphlet claimed they were made from a fabric that was "unsurpassed for sweat management."

Sweat management!

Phil's two-word note read, "Panty hose."

One of these days, if I think of it, I'll give them a try.

Chapter Nineteen

Why Knot?

Angling knots are like basketball referees—as long as they're doing a good job, you don't notice them.

But when your line suddenly goes limp a few minutes after you've sunk your hook into the jaw of the biggest brown trout of your life, you don't even have to look to know what happened. Bad knot. Bust-offs always happen at knots. They're the weakest links in that long thin chain from your hand to the fish.

The fault could be with how you tied that knot. Or you might've tied an unsuitable knot perfectly. Not all knots are equal. Some knots, no matter how well they're tied, will not do the job. Either way, when a knot fails, it's your fault. I hate it when that happens.

Fishermen have to know how to tie knots that a normal person can live an entire lifetime without needing. Who besides a fisherman has ever even heard of a Huffnagle knot?

On the other hand, a square knot will not hold two pieces of monofilament together, and there is no known angling use for a bow knot. It won't even keep your wading boots tied up.

When I was a kid and showed some inclination to like fishing, my father sat me down in the living room and handed me two lengths of old fly line. "If you want to be a fisherman," he said, "you've got to tie your own knots." He showed me how to make a blood knot and I had to practice it until he saw that I could do it by myself. Then he made me learn the Turle—"Not 'turtle,'" he emphasized—knot.

"As soon as you can tie two pieces of leader together and tie a fly onto the end of your tippet," he said, "you can go fishing with me, because I'm not going to tie your knots for you."

It wasn't until I started taking my own kids fishing with me that I understood his reasoning.

I once fished a famous Rocky Mountain trout river with a hovering guide. He followed me around, stood at my elbow, and kept up a steady stream of advice. He told me where to stand, where to cast, when to mend my line, when to lift and cast again, and in general managed to take all the fun out of it. Otherwise, he was a pretty nice guy, though, and I didn't have the heart to tell him to go away and leave me alone until he grabbed my leader and started to change flies for me. That's when I asked him to run back to the boat and fetch my camera.

The last time I allowed somebody else to tie on my fly, I hooked a good fish, busted it off, and brought in a leader with a pigtail on the end. For some reason, I found this less acceptable than if I'd tied that bad knot myself.

Some fishermen collect knots the way they collect hopper patterns. They can show you how to tie dozens of different ones. This is entirely harmless, of course, but I've never understood the purpose of knowing how to tie inherently weak knots.

People like to invent knots and name them after themselves. This is a good way to become immortal. Otherwise, who would've ever heard of Major Turle? Or, for that matter, Mr. Huffnagle? George Harvey and Homer Rhode and Jimmie Albright have solidified their places in angling history by inventing knots. So have people named Duncan and Crawford.

A good rule is: Never trust knots named after people. They are either too fancy or too unreliable.

I can't tie any useful knots with my eyes closed, although there are plenty of times when I wish I could. It's hard enough to tie a good knot with a mini-flashlight clenched in my teeth and mosquitoes swarming about my face and trout rising all around me.

Most knots require a minimum of three forefingers and four thumbs to tie. If you are one of those people who were born with only two hands, you'll need to develop dexterity with your lips, tongue, and teeth.

There are a lot of knot-tying tools on the market. I've tried many of them, but I've never been able to follow the directions.

A good knot should be close to 100 percent strong—that is, as strong as the leader it's tied with. It should be easy and quick to make. You should be able to form it perfectly without thinking about what you're doing. Your mind would rather be planning your next cast.

Lubricating them with saliva before pulling them tight makes all knots stronger. The gunky stuff you hack up from your throat works better than the spit from your mouth. This is a useful tip that has never before been published.

Most of us would rather fish than tie knots. The more complicated the knot, the less likely we are to take a time-out from fishing to tie it. Knowing only complicated knots discourages us from changing flies or remaking a short or weakened leader.

Before I learned the surgeon's knot, I'd do almost anything to avoid changing or adding tippet. I'd end up with a five-foot leader tapered to about 1X. I knew why I wasn't catching any trout, but I preferred not catching trout to the agonizing frustration of rebuilding my leader. That blood knot my father taught me makes an artful connection, and I know guides who can tie one in about five seconds. I can't. Mine keep pulling loose.

I taught the surgeon's knot to my friend Dr. Andrew Warshaw, who is the chief of surgery at Mass. General Hospital. He'd never heard of it.

It was gratifying to hear Lefty say that the surgeon's knot is close to 100 percent efficient. But even if it weren't, I'd probably still use it.

For tying all but tiny flies to spiderweb tippets, I use the trilene knot, which I'd like even better if it weren't named after a commercial product associated with spinfishing. The key to the trilene knot is poking the end of the tippet through the hook eye twice. Otherwise it's a clinch knot, which is about as simple as a knot gets. When I can't squeeze a 6X tippet through a No. 20

hook eye twice, in fact, the clinch knot is what I use. I know that an "improved" clinch knot is, well, an improvement. But it's just fussy enough to make me settle for the unimproved version. If I resolved to improve all my clinch knots, I'd change flies less frequently.

For joining a leader butt to the end of a fly line, you've got to be able to tie a nail knot. There are about a dozen variations on the nail knot, and it doesn't require an actual nail. It can be tied with matchsticks, twigs, drinking straws, needles, and fly-tying bobbins. My friend Bill Rohrbacher can tie one in the dark with black caddis crawling into his eyes in about a minute. He uses no implement whatsoever. For most of us, though, the nail knot is best tied at home, in the den, with the door closed and the stereo turned up loud so the kids can't hear us.

A drop of superglue makes all the difference with a nail knot.

My angling partner, Andy Gill, prefers to attach his flies to his tippet with a loop knot. He contends that a loop rather than a snugged-down connection between the tippet and the eye of the hook maximizes the action of the fly in the water, reduces what he calls "micro drag" with small dry flies, and prevents the leader from twisting and kinking when he's casting airplanelike spinners. Lefty rates the nonslip mono loop pretty high for strength, and it's not too fussy. I'm trying to get into the habit of using it for spinners, at least. But when I'm standing in a pool full of dimpling trout, my mind is on other things, and I usually end up with a clinch knot.

The wind knot is extremely popular among fly fishermen. Its most important use is to give the angler an excuse for busting off a fish.

The wind knot is a simple overhand knot, and even a beginner can master it in an afternoon on the water. The best way to tie wind knots is to cast a tailing loop. They are hardly ever actually tied by the wind. Wind knots are so easy to make that I often find I've tied several of them without even trying.

Part V

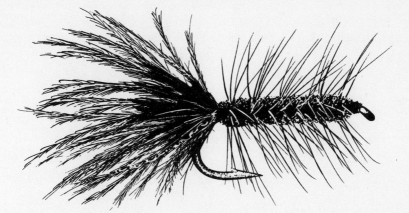

The Fly-Tying Fallacy

"**A** fly is not a fly at all. It is something which, in the conversation of a fisherman, is referred to as such—but nothing is further from the truth! The standard materials used in fly tying are, first, the hook, consisting of three prime parts: The eye (to which the leader is attached), the shank (to which the body or general dressing is attached), and the barb, to which, it is hoped, a large fish will eventually be attached; and the second, the dressing, consisting of the hair of many animals, the feathers of many fowls, and tinsel of many varieties. These, and sometimes a great many other materials, are wound with silk thread upon the hook and the result is beautiful to behold."

—Edmund Ware Smith

quoted in *The Fly Tyer's Handbook,* by H. G. Tapply (1949)

Chapter Twenty

Simplify, Simplify

June on the Vineyard. Prime striper time, and we are there, six of us, the five shrinks and I. Toward dusk we hit the beaches—Lobsterville and Dogfish Bar, or, depending on the wind, maybe down the other end of the island at Wasque or Cape Pogue. If the tide is ebbing, State Beach might be hot at the jetties where the ponds empty into the sea. We consult local oracles and make our own best guesses, and sometimes second guesses after it's too late.

We fish till midnight, stagger back to the cottage, sleep for a couple of hours, and then stumble out there again to beat the sunrise.

We are middle-aged, sedentary men, accustomed to office hours and regular, civilized schedules, and after a day or two of this madness, we become cranky and bleary. We could, of course, sleep during the time of high sun. But we don't. As Andy likes to say, "The Big Sleep will come soon enough. Meanwhile, are we here to relax, or to fish?"

So when we aren't actually fishing, we are preparing to fish. Usually that means tying flies to match what we think the stripers are eating. It doesn't matter that each of us brings a dozen boxes crammed with flies of every size, color, shape, and design, or that we've been tying for months in preparation for this trip. When we actually get here, we inevitably worry that we are undersupplied.

Jon is usually the first one to empty his portable fly-tying kit onto the dining room table, set up his vise, clamp in a stainless-steel hook, and start rummaging among his materials. He's muttering, "Sand eels."

Nontiers Steve and Randy lean over Jon's shoulders. "What're you making?" "What's that stuff?" "Hey, will you make one of them for me?"

Elliot is next. He mumbles "Corsair and epoxy," digs into his duffel bag, and then his vise is set up. Andy, as competitive in fly tying as he is in fly fishing, can't resist. He's got a killer sand eel pattern in mind, his own variation of a complex, multimaterial design he read about somewhere.

The Fly-Tying Fallacy

—

I fight it for a while, but eventually I sigh, drain my coffee mug, retrieve my traveling fly-tying kit, and wedge myself into an opening around the table.

Steve finds some blues on the radio. Randy refills the coffeepot. The rest of us bend silently to our vises.

After a while, Elliot crows, "Lookit this." He passes around his sand eel fly. "Careful," he says. "The epoxy's still tacky." We handle his fly by the hook bend, and we all agree that it is elegant and complicated and altogether imitative. An admirable effort and a certain striper slayer.

A few minutes later, Andy's got one done, and even Elliot concedes that Andy's fly looks more like a sand eel than his— more, maybe, than even an actual sand eel.

By now I've tied six sand eel flies. I lean back, stretch and yawn ostentatiously, and hand two of my creations to Steve and another two to Randy. "Here you go," I say. "Guaranteed to nail you a cow. Don't bust 'em off."

Steve squints at the flies I've given him. They are dark olive, more or less the color of the sand eels that are hatching along the Vineyard beaches. They are slender and plenty wiggly. "Cool," says Steve. "What do you call it?"

"Woolly Bugger," I reply.

"I knew that," says Steve. "Freshwater fly, isn't it?"

"Not necessarily."

* * *

Elliot and Andy might disagree, but when it comes to tying flies that will surely catch fish, I subscribe to Thoreau's dictum: "Simplify, simplify." Good—but hard-to-follow—advice for living one's life, and even better—and much easier-to-follow—advice for creating flies that predatory saltwater fish will eat.

You can't get much simpler than a Woolly Bugger.

If the purpose of tying flies were to produce guaranteed fish catchers, and do it quickly, cheaply, and with minimal skill, I'd simply fill my saltwater boxes with Woolly Buggers.

I'd tie 'em on small (No. 6), medium (No. 2), and large (No. 2/0) hooks, and in light (beige and white), medium (olive and chartreuse), and dark (black and purple) colors. I'd make 'em fat and bushy, sparse and slender, and in between. I'd add lead eyes to some of them, and maybe some glitter to their tails. I'd end up with several dozen Woolly Buggers, and I'd feel utterly confident that I could catch whatever briny gamefish I sought under any condition.

And if none of those worked, some other Bugger in a different size, shape, and/or color would do the job. Guaranteed.

The Fly-Tying Fallacy

For most saltwater fly fishing most of the time, the fly we tie on is the least important variable. Far more crucial are locating the fish, stalking to within casting range without spooking them, casting the fly quickly and accurately, showing it to them where they can see it, and retrieving it so that it looks alive, edible, and vulnerable. Just tie on a Woolly Bugger, fish it properly, and don't worry about imitation. Do this, and few saltwater fish will question what species of prey your fly's intended to imitate.

Most of us have moved to fly fishing in the brine from trout streams. We recognize and appreciate the selective nature of trout, and we want flies that closely imitate the species and emergence stage of the insect that we find trout keying on. We know that at least sometimes, the difference between success and failure can be the length of the trailing shuck on our emerger or the shade of rust in the body of our spinner.

When we embrace saltwater fly fishing, we tend to impute the same "thinking" to striped bass—and tarpon, bonefish, redfish, and blues. We feel more confident if we believe we've "matched the hatch." We can't help it—it's that old trout conditioning.

Sometimes, in fact, we're sort of right. We know that stripers, for example, gluttonize on sand eels, cinderworms, shrimp, or soft-shelled lobsters, or silversides, herring, or pogies, whenever those prey are abundant. Bonefish gobble shrimp and permit eat crabs off the bottom of tropical flats. Under these conditions, a fly that more or less resembles what they're eating, presented at the proper depth, and retrieved in a manner imitative of the way that prey behaves, is your best bet to catch fish.

In fact, a Woolly Bugger can be made to resemble almost any critter a saltwater fish might be looking for.

Baitfish? Match the size and color and add a few strands of Krystal Flash to the tail, eyes up front, and maybe a few turns of red hackle behind the eyes to suggest gills.

Sand eel? Half a sprig of olive marabou, olive body, just a few turns of slim grizzly hackle.

Shrimp? Lead eyes on top of the hook shank (to tip the fly over so it won't foul on the bottom, where it should be fished), stubby beige or olive tail (depending on the bottom you're fishing over), matching body and hackle.

Cinderworm? Orange marabou, ginger hackle, and orange body. Make it sexy with a few turns of dark brown chenille at the head.

Lobster? Tie it big and mingle brown and dark olive marabou, olive body, bushy mixed brown and olive hackle. Trim the hackle into a body shape.

Squid? Big and white, with an extra-long tail and black eyes mounted over the bend of the hook.

Crab? Make it short and fat, palmer on four or five hackles instead of one, then clip the top and bottom flat.

What have I left out?

* * *

Of course, showing them something entirely different from what's most abundant is often the best way to catch the biggest fish in the vicinity. Something like a Woolly Bugger.

* * *

My daughter Sarah was six years old and had been watching me tie flies for a couple of years before she said she wanted to try it. So I patted my lap, and up she climbed. I showed her how to make a half-hitch and keep tension on the thread, then watched her tie a Woolly Bugger that looked pretty much like the ones I'd been making (except hers featured a pink tail, chartreuse body, and yellow hackle). I dubbed it the Pink Sarah, assured her it would catch fish, and a few months later when she trolled it past a hungry smallmouth bass, it did.

Randy and Steve and other nontiers of my acquaintance marvel at the dexterity and artistry of those of us who insist on fishing with flies we've made ourselves. We, of course, like to promote the illusion. It looks difficult, they think, so they buy and bum flies—and they miss out on the special kick we get from catching fish on our own creations.

But there is no reason why anybody, no matter how banana-fingered and unimaginative, shouldn't supply himself with proven fish takers. Money? If you consider the cost of saltwater flies (anywhere from $2.50 to $6 apiece in most catalogs and shops), the simple materials and tools you need for tying Buggers will repay you very soon.

Time? I can tie a dozen Woolly Buggers in an hour, and I'm fairly banana-fingered.

Creativity? You don't need any imagination whatsoever to follow a simple three-step recipe and turn out a Woolly Bugger.

Skill? If six-year-old Sarah (and I) can do it, anybody can.

* * *

But wait. You've peeked into my saltwater fly boxes. You've discovered Deceivers, Clousers, Whistlers, and Slab Flies. There are epoxy flies, Corsair flies, poppers, sliders, coneheads, and woolheads; and in another box you find Gotchas, Crazy Charlies, MOEs, Merkins, McCrabs, and Puffs. My freshwater streamer boxes are equally crammed.

You also see dozens of flies that resemble nothing you've ever seen before, weird combinations of materials, colors, and designs that have no names and probably never will.

Okay, you found me out: I do not rely exclusively on Woolly Buggers. Never said I did. I only said I *could*. This has been a conditional argument. *If,* I said, all you wanted to do was supply yourself with guaranteed fish takers, and *if* you cherished factors such as efficiency and practicality, *then,* I said, tie Woolly Buggers and you'd be all set.

I'll stick by my premise. But inevitably, it seems, even the most practical fly tier surrenders to his curiosity, imagination, and creativity. There are new materials to play with, old tying tricks to try in a new way, variations on proven patterns, and unproven creations you'd like to prove.

Pretty soon, it's not enough to catch fish on flies you've tied yourself. You want to catch fish on flies you've invented. And somewhere along the line, tying ceases to be an efficient, economical, and practical way to stock your fly boxes. It becomes as integral to your fishing experience as analyzing tide and forecasting weather, stalking and casting, hooking and landing. Fly tying, in fact, becomes like fishing itself: expensive, time consuming, and altogether obsessive.

* * *

Assemble your own travel kit, and regardless of how many hundreds of excellent flies you already have with you, you can't resist dumping your stuff out on the table at your rented cottage. Picture those stripers, gobbling sand eels along the beaches. Rummage through your materials. Stare out the window, sip your coffee, hum along with the old bluesman on the radio. Daydream for a while before you start lashing stuff onto the hook. You might discard one, two, ten attempts before you're finally convinced that you've created a fly no one has ever seen before, a fly that has no name, but a fly that will surely mimic those little sand eels better than a sand eel itself. *Your* fly. *Your* invention.

You're hooked, pal. Just don't blame me. I told you to stick to Woolly Buggers.

Chapter Twenty-one

Bill's Bow-Tie Dun (Patent Pending)

New flies are being invented daily, it seems. Open any fly-fishing catalog and you'll find at least one page heralding exciting new patterns and design concepts that are guaranteed to catch fish that hitherto could not be caught. Just about every issue of every fly-fishing magazine on the market contains an article announcing the creation of a brand-new fly that will solve previously unsolvable angling conundrums.

Often the claims for these new flies are modest: "The Reversed-Hackle No-Body Crippled Dun is just the ticket for those times when trout are sipping *Baetis* spinners with broken left wings."

Sometimes the claims are downright mouthwatering: "Just throw the all-new Twister-Tail Nymerging-Spinnerdun anywhere onto the water. Even if you can't cast, you'll catch fish, guaranteed. This amazing fly does all the work."

The evidence for the magical properties of the new fly generally takes the form of an anecdote: "Trout were boiling all over the Middle Fork of the Big Hard-Hearted River, but no one was catching anything. I kept changing flies, but nothing worked, and I was ready to call it a day. Then I remembered the Inside-Out Crippled Drifter. The inspiration for this unique fly had come to me at three-thirty on a cold February morning when a dream about being immersed in a spring creek of single malt and breathing through gills had awakened me in a sweat. I crawled out of bed and dragged myself to my tying vise, and before I knew it, the IOCD had materialized before my bleary eyes.

"Anyway, I tied on the IOCD with no expectation, but I hooked a six-pound brown on the first cast. Before darkness fell that evening, I had landed forty-two trout, the smallest of which was twenty-five inches long. Nobody else caught anything. Since that eye-opening experience, the IOCD is the only fly I ever use, and I always outfish everybody."

The Fly-Tying Fallacy

Well, inventing and experimenting is part of the fun of fly fishing, and there's no question that every one of these new designs will catch fish. I've found twigs, pebbles, and cigarette filters in the stomachs of large trout. Trout explore their world with their mouths the way toddlers paw through displays of feminine hygiene products in the supermarket. Curiosity has probably killed as many trout as hunger.

Most fly-tying anglers of my acquaintance harbor secret dreams of immortality. They yearn to be the Lee of the Wulff series, the Dave of Hopper fame, the Royal Coachman himself, and they imagine scenarios played out while watching the water from the banks of, say, the Henry's Fork:

Stranger: Hi, there. How they biting?

Angler: Oh, I'm doin' okay. You?

Stranger: Haven't raised a thing. These are tough fish. My name's Mike, by the way.

Angler: Mike? Mike Lawson? The guru of the Henry's Fork? You the guy who runs the fly shop, writes those articles, gives those fly-tying demonstrations?

Lawson: That's me.

Angler: No luck, huh?

Lawson: One of those Henry's Fork days, I guess.

Angler (holding out his hand): It's an honor to meet you. I'm Felix.

Lawson (mouth dropping open): Not *the* Felix? You're not by chance the Felix who invented Felix's Blue-Collar Semi-Shuck Emerger?

Felix (modestly): Well, yes. I am.

Lawson (eagerly): Oh, boy. This is a thrill. Listen, Felix. I've organized a seminar for advanced anglers from all over the world. We gather next week, and I'd be honored if you'd consent to be our keynote speaker. I've got Lefty Kreh lined up now, but I know when he hears I had the chance to get you he'll understand. What's your customary fee?

If you tie flies, you probably fiddle around with materials and proportions. Is there a tier anywhere who hasn't dubbed a nymph with the fuzzy fur from his wife's cat's belly or made a hopper body from a piece of Styrofoam coffee cup? The creative impulse drives us all, and sometimes our inventions work almost as well as the old standards.

But an Elkhair Caddis or a Pheasant-Tail Nymph doesn't come along every day. True breakthroughs in trout-fly design happen maybe once every generation.

The Fly-Tying Fallacy

—

I mention all this so you'll know I'm not naive. Sure, like everybody else, I've always secretly harbored fantasies of angling immortality. The fact is, I've invented dozens of flies, and I've caught fish on all of them. But before I came up with Bill's Bow-Tie Dun, I never thought any of them deserved to be named after me.

A fly worthy of my name had to be more than a variation on some tired old theme. Substituting a different feather or animal's fur on a tried-and-true pattern might make a marginally better fly, but I was aiming higher.

Bill's Bow-Tie Dun was no accident, no whim, no fluke, no daydreamy by-product of hacking around at the vise. I wanted something that would spare me—and fly tiers everywhere—the aggravation of winding hackles and cocking wings and all that other fussy nonsense that virtually all dry-fly patterns require, and that have always made fly tying an exercise in frustration for me.

The solution came to me only after years of analysis, trial, and error. I raised mayflies in my home aquarium, snorkeled upside down in my local trout streams (a feat in itself, but the only way to get the trout's perspective), read every book ever published on the subject of aquatic insects and their imitations, and experimented with fly-tying materials and techniques before all those hours of effort finally paid off, and I came up with—dare I say it?—an absolutely *revolutionary* design.

Like most wonderful new inventions, the genius of Bill's Bow-Tie Dun lies in its obvious, albeit elegant, simplicity. When its secret is revealed, I know, you'll slap your forehead and mutter: "Why didn't *I* think of that?"

Well, you didn't. I did. Eat your heart out.

This is what I did. It was about as easy as tying my shoes:

1. I tied on a tail, dubbed a body all the way to the front, built up the thorax, and finished with a half-hitch. I left the tying silk hanging about a quarter of the way back on the shank.

2. I cut a six-inch length of grayish, mayfly-wing-colored poly yarn. Then I rotated my vise so I was looking at the hook straight-on. Now here's the secret of Bill's Bow-Tie Dun: I tied the poly yarn on over the thorax *with a bow knot!* The two bows were the fly's wings. I tugged on the ends of the yarn to get the the bows even and then tightened the knot by pulling simultaneously on the two bows, which sat cocked on the top of the hook. The two long ends angled downward.

3. I trimmed the two ends so they were about three-eighths of an inch long, and when I combed them out, the poly yarn flared like hackle fibers. To my eye, it mimicked a mayfly's legs and looked like it would support the fly in the water.

4. I finished the fly by figure-eighting the thread around the two bow "wings" and through the poly "hackles," formed a neat head, and added a drop of cement to both the knot and the head.

Eureka!

The poly yarn wings and legs have that translucent, light-gathering look that hair and feathers never quite achieve. The fly itself cocks up prettily in the palm of my hand, and—the moment of truth—it floats perkily in a saucer of water.

Will it catch fish?

That's hardly relevant. Anything will catch fish. But I can tell you this: Bill's Bow-Tie Dun looks a helluva lot better than a cigarette filter.

Chapter Twenty-two

Fly-Tying Season

The smells—mothballs and head cement and dye bubbling on the stove—are evocative for me still. So are the names—jungle cock, golden pheasant, peacock; tinsel, floss, chenille; blue dun, ginger, grizzly. After half a century, I still can't sit down to tie a fly without remembering . . .

In my family, the fly-tying season opened the day after the duck season closed, and it ended when the ice went out on Sebago Lake to signal the beginning of landlocked salmon fishing. Every year on New Year's Day, my father set up his fly-tying bench in the living room, and he sat at it just about every winter evening. When I was a boy, I liked to pull up a chair by his elbow to watch him tie while *I Love Lucy* aired in another corner of the room.

After dinner he laid out the materials for the evening, and I soon learned that the brown bucktail and the skein of yellow chenille meant an evening of Dark Tigers, while the grizzly and ginger necks and the wood-duck flank feathers meant that a couple dozen spent-wing Adamses would magically emerge from Dad's vise. When he took out the big hooks and opened the green breadbox that held his bucktails and deer hides, I knew it would be an evening of what he called "hedge trimming"—spinning and clipping deer-hair bass bugs.

He never used a bobbin. He stripped off a couple of feet of tying silk, ran it through his ball of beeswax, and used a half-hitch to secure the thread after each operation. He spread a dish towel on his lap to collect the trimmings, and after a session at the bench, he folded up the towel, went out to the front porch, and dumped the clippings onto the snow. "The birds will find it when the snow melts," he said. "They'll use it for their nests."

He was right. Come spring, I liked to wander around the yard looking for the bird nests, and they always had strands of yellow chenille, silver tinsel, and bits of bucktail and hackle feathers woven into them.

The Fly-Tying Fallacy

—

My father supplied his nontying friends with flies, and since he had many friends, every winter he tied tens of dozens of flies—flies for every angling occasion, flies that his friends requested, flies for his friends' friends. Nobody paid him, nor did he want them to. They gave him back in companionship what he gave them in flies.

He tied commercially for a while in the early 1940s. "Three for a dollar was the going rate," he remembers. "It was a hard way to make money, and I didn't do it for very long. My problem was, I was a perfectionist. I refused to sell a fly with any flaw, even if no one would notice it except me. But I learned a lot about fly tying that way, and I ended up with an awful lot of flawed flies. They all caught fish."

He approached fly tying as a manufacturing process, and he called it a craft. But to me, what he did was an art, and the pieces he created were beautiful: perfectly symmetrical and proportioned, smoothly tapered, subtly colored. When I watched him, he made it look easy.

As the winter nights passed, his boxes filled with flies. There were few evenings when Dad didn't put in an hour or two at the vise.

And if I sat there quietly and waited long enough, he'd eventually pat his knee and invite me to climb up and try it. I'm positive I was the only kid in my second-grade class who could roll a wood-duck wing and wind a hackle feather and make a whip-finish.

My flies never looked like Dad's, as hard as I tried. The wings always flared out at odd angles, and the heads came out big and lumpy. But when I finished my evening's fly and took it from the vise and handed it to my father, he always held it up, squinted at it, poked it with his finger, and then handed it back to me. "Yup," he always said. "This one'll catch fish, all right."

Through the months of the fly-tying season, my own little box of flies slowly filled, and when the fishing season arrived, I tried them and discovered that Dad was right: As flawed and amateurish and outlandishly designed as my creations were, they *did* catch fish.

I gradually figured out that *anything* would catch fish if you tied it onto your leader and kept it in the water long enough.

Dad tied flies to suit the angling situations the years had taught him to expect. He loved making streamers best, perhaps because well-tied streamers are graceful and beautiful to look at, or perhaps because tying them evoked memories of trolling for landlocked salmon on Moosehead and Sebago right after ice-out, which he loved, and which was the first fishing he did every spring. The Dark Edson Tiger was his favorite, but he tied Grey Ghosts, Supervisors, and Warden's Worries, plus dozens of variations on those patterns and many pure inventions of his own. He fished with all of them, and they all caught fish, of course.

It occurred to me that he could've named dozens of his gorgeous and unique landlocked salmon streamers and bucktails after himself, thereby securing a little piece of angling immortality for his name, as many of his friends did.

But that wasn't Tap.

* * *

H. G. Tapply wrote a column called "The Sportsman's Notebook" plus six "Tap's Tips" for *Field & Stream* every month for thirty-five years. That added up to more than twenty-five hundred fifty-word tips plus nearly five hundred articles, many of which addressed fly fishing, fly design, and fly tying. Millions of outdoorsmen considered Tap their wise and trusted mentor. He had abundant opportunity to make himself famous.

But he always said, "Oh, I'm no expert."

He invented many flies. Every invention was calculated to solve a practical angling problem. His landlocked salmon streamers were designed to imitate the smelt that made up the main diet of ice-out salmon. He tied dry flies to suggest the mayflies and caddisflies he found trout eating on his local streams. His deer-hair bass bugs were intended to cast comfortably on a medium-weight fly rod, to float like corks, and to kick up a strike-inducing ruckus on the water.

He once handed me a big yellow bucktail tied on an extra-long-shanked hook. "Pickerel fly," he said. "No body. On account of their teeth."

I told him I thought he might have a good article in that idea. "You could call it Tap's Pickerel Special," I said.

He smiled. "It would be a damn short article."

He tied flies to catch fish. He knew, of course, that anything would catch fish if you kept it in the water long enough. But he also believed that a well-conceived and neatly tied fly would catch more and bigger fish.

The only fly he ever bothered giving a name to was the Nearenuf. Not "Tap's Nearenuf." Just the Nearenuf. It combined elements of the important eastern mayfly hatches he fished to—hendricksons, quill gordons, March browns, and light cahills. The Nearenuf didn't look exactly like any of them, but it was, he figured, near enough.

He was a stout believer in the importance of presentation and suggestion, and he scoffed at those who worried about the number of fibers in the tail or the shade of olive on the body of a mayfly imitation. He thought that fishermen should spend less time agonizing over fly selection and knot tying and more time drifting a fly on the water. He invented the Nearenuf to test his belief, and he convinced his fishing partners to join him in a season-long experiment. He supplied them with a year's supply of Nearenufs on the condition that they'd fish only with them, keep a record of their success, and then compare the results to previous years of hatch matching.

Not surprisingly, they did as well with the Nearenuf as they ever had done. I liked to tell Dad that if Tup could have an Indispensable, surely Tap could have a Nearenuf. He just laughed. He'd made his point.

He invented a deer-hair bass bug that still cannot be surpassed. It's a model of simplicity—a sprig of deer hair for a tail and a tightly packed spun deer-hair body trimmed to a wedge shape with a flat face. It casts like a bullet and goes *ploop* and *gurgle* when it's retrieved, and I haven't met a bass that can resist it. Dan Bailey's catalog carried this bug for years. It eventu-

ally became known as "Tap's Bug"—but that was the name
others gave it.

* * *

Tap was self-taught. "By the middle of the nineteen-thirties
sometime," he remembers, "I'd gotten pretty serious about fly
fishing. Flies were expensive, so I decided I better learn to tie my
own. Back then, there was only one book that I knew of for beginners. It was called *How to Tie Flies* by E. C. Gregg. I read it
and reread it and struggled to understand it. The problem with
Mr. Gregg's book was, it told you *what* to do, but it didn't tell you
how to do it. I ended up learning mostly by trial and error. After I
figured it out and got so I could tie a pretty good fly, I remembered how much a clearly written beginner's manual would've
helped me. So I wrote *The Fly Tyer's Handbook* while I still remembered all the problems I'd faced when I was trying to learn."

The *Handbook* first appeared in a cheap paperback edition in
the early 1940s and was reprinted in hardcover in 1949. It has
been out of print for decades, of course. But even a reporter less
biased than Tap's son would be hard pressed to find a clearer,
more useful, or more encouraging manual for beginners.

"I often wonder why more fishermen don't embrace [fly tying]
as a hobby," he wrote. "Perhaps the reason lies in the common

fallacy that tying flies is a difficult art. But it isn't. If you have a full complement of fingers in good working order and enough perseverance to see a thing through, you can learn to tie surprisingly good flies in a surprisingly short period of time."

Or: "Fly tying must be learned the hard way—through practice. There are, however, a few methods and kinks that will prove immensely helpful to the beginner. That is why I believe this chapter [in which he provided lucid instructions on tying the half-hitch and the whip-finish, among other things] should be the most valuable of the entire book; learning how to make fly tying easier by using the simplest and most amateur-proof methods will save the beginner much discouragement and start him tying creditable flies in a reasonably short time."

He remembered what it was like to be starting out, and he made no assumptions: "The first and most obvious step in fly tying is to insert the hook in the vise—an act, however, that is not quite so simple as it sounds."

* * *

Tap continued to tie flies for his friends well into his eighties, even after he'd grown too lame and wobbly to wade a stream or paddle a canoe.

Then came the day when he bequeathed all of his fly-tying tools and materials to me. "Take it," he said, waving his hand at the boxes, envelopes, bags, and cabinets that he'd stacked beside the door. "I can't use it anymore."

I knelt down, opened the old green breadbox, and sniffed the mothballed bucktails. I prowled through the bags, boxes, and envelopes, and found jungle cock, golden pheasant, and peacock, tinsel, chenille, and floss, blue dun, ginger, and grizzly necks. I looked up at him. "You sure?"

He held up his hands and wiggled his gnarled, swollen, arthritic fingers. "Alas," he said, "I no longer have a full complement of fingers in good working order."

Part VI

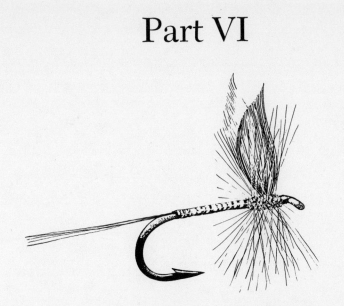

Life as a Metaphor for Fly Fishing

"**N**ot everything about fishing is noble and reasonable and sane. . . . Fishing is not an escape from life, but often a deeper immersion into it, all of it, the good and the awful, the joyous and the miserable, the comic, the embarrassing, the tragic, and the sorrowful."

—Harry Middleton
Rivers of Memory (1993)

Chapter Twenty-three

Timing

I'd always thought that sanity was more or less a prerequisite for anyone who practiced psychiatry. I'm not sure why I thought that. I mean, we don't expect television evangelists to practice sound morals or lawyers actually to obey the law. But it had always seemed to me that doctors of the human psyche would, by both their character and their training, ooze rationality, calmness, and common sense. A conversation with a shrink, I thought, would be characterized by long moments of thoughtful silence punctuated now and then by softly spoken words of wisdom, insight, and perspective.

Andy Gill set me straight. We had met a few times around town, talked a little baseball, debated the best hot stuff for chili, agreed that bourbon was superior to Scotch and that diet soda tasted funny—and that we both liked fly fishing. Andy was a shrink, and those casual encounters only reinforced my concept of what a psychiatrist should be.

We kept saying that we ought to go fishing together some time, and I think we both meant it. But our lives were complicated and busy, and neither of us seemed able to come up with a specific date that worked for both of us.

Then one July afternoon Andy came banging at my door. His eyes were blazing and his hands were waving in the air. "It's *hot!*" he kept saying. "We gotta go *now!*"

I took his arm and steered him to a rocking chair on my front porch. "Calm down," I murmured soothingly. "Why don't you tell me about it."

"Omigod," he sputtered. "You should've been there. I mean, you *gotta* do this. You owe it to yourself. You owe it to *me*. Time's a-wasting, you know? Life is short. Carpe diem, man."

I stroked my chin. "Mmm," I said. "Can you recall when you began feeling this way?"

"Brown trout like *this*." He held his hands about two feet apart. "Huge pods of 'em with their shoulders out of water like *sharks*, man, and PMDs hatching all day, then toward dusk the black caddis . . ."

"Okay, okay," I said. "Sounds good. Let's do it some time."

Andy's knee was jiggling so fast it was a blur, and I thought he was going to rock himself right through the screens. "Not some time," he said. "*Now!* We can't wait. It's not gonna last. Nothing does. If we don't do it—"

"We'll do it," I said.

And we did, and the Bighorn was everything Andy had said it would be: The pale morning duns began to pop at eleven every morning, and they lasted all day until they merged into the black caddis hatch toward evening, and we moved from pod to pod of rising fish, picking them off.

When you're actually there, and when it's perfect, you're convinced it will always be that way. We had discovered dry-fly Nirvana, and we vowed to return every year for the rest of our lives.

For a long time, I didn't understand Andy's jittery urgency. We kept questing for new waters to explore, and it seemed that we just kept discovering other Nirvanas. When we fished the Frying Pan River in October, we found it full of piggy rainbows shaped like rugby balls, and we caught them on No. 22 midge pupae tied to long 6X tippets. Each of us landed an eight-pounder on that trip. We fished Utah's Green River in June during the cicada "hatch" and caught so many big trout on dry flies that resembled tarantulas that we actually got tired of it.

Andy and I trekked to a little pond in Centennial Valley and found leg-sized trout sipping *Callibaetis* duns. We caught muscular rainbows from the dependable Madison, and when we kept missing the salmonfly hatch, we vowed to time it better next year. We failed to hit the green drakes on the Henry's Fork, but we did learn why it's legendary. We fell in love with DePuy Spring Creek. We caught winter steelhead from New York's Salmon River, and Andy even landed a coho salmon from the Indian Head River on the Massachusetts South Shore.

The world, I believed, was full of wonderful fishing, and I found the memory of all those great places and the anticipation of revisiting them almost as pleasant as actually being there.

I liked a big steak at the end of a long day, a good night's sleep, a leisurely breakfast. I liked sitting on the riverbank looking at the mountains and watching the birds and savoring it all. But Andy never calmed down. He fished hard and long and intensely, and when he wasn't fishing, he jittered and jiggled and worried about where we should go next. He fished as if every river would dry up tomorrow, as if every trout he cast to was the last one on earth.

Life as a Metaphor for Fly Fishing

—

"Slow down," I kept telling him. "Take your time."

"That's just it," he'd say. "Time is our enemy."

"You could at least relax once in a while."

"Oh, we'll do that," he'd say. "When the Big Sleep comes we can catch up on all that relaxing. But meanwhile, we gotta fish."

Then disturbing, unpredicted things began to happen. The coho salmon stopped returning to the Indian Head River, whirling disease struck the Madison, and they drained the pond with the leg-long trout in the Centennial Valley. For a while, the PMDs stopped hatching on the Bighorn, and when they returned, they came in unpredictable spurts according to the whim of those who decided when to release water from the Yellowtail Dam. Cicadas, we discovered, did not "hatch" every year along the banks of the Green, and those butterball rainbows disappeared from the Frying Pan when the mysis shrimp that had nourished them disappeared from the reservoir above the Reudi Dam. The flood of the century swept away DePuy Spring Creek. The steelhead population in the Salmon River crashed. Even the Henry's Fork seemed to have lost its luster.

Andy and I began to find ourselves in the wrong places at the wrong times. And when that happened, he'd moan: "See? This is what I've been trying to tell you. It's all about timing. Now, I just read about this lake in Wyoming, see, and it's full of monster rainbows. I mean eight-, ten-pounders. They come into the shallows in June to gobble damselfly nymphs, and you can sight-fish 'em like bonefish, and it's hot *right now*, and it ain't gonna last . . ."

"Things change." "Life is short." "Timing is everything." "Seize the day." "Strike while the iron is hot." "The early bird gets the worm." These are clichés because they are so true as to be self-evident.

As I write this, my New England coastal waters are swarming with striped bass as never before in recorded history. It's there for me, anytime I want it—except now I know that it's *not*. It will not last. Nothing does. The fabled Catskill streams sure ain't what they used to be, and Atlantic salmon have disappeared from New England coastal rivers. Even the little meadow stream that harbored native brookies when I was a kid now flows warm and muddy through a concrete trough behind a shopping mall.

I've learned to forgo sleeping, eating, nursing important relationships, and earning a living to be wherever it's happening during this eye blink of time that's mine, thanks to Andy—who's turned out to be the sanest man I know.

* * *

Life as a Metaphor for Fly Fishing

—

201

He called me this morning. "Carpe diem, baby!" he said. He was sputtering, and I could practically feel his knee jiggling.

"I know," I said. "Seize the day. Good advice. You taught me that, and I agree."

"Yeah, that too. But what I mean is, today's a good day to go carp fishing. It's carp day, see? I just heard about this section of the Charles River where huge carp cruise the shoreline and eat dry flies, and you *know* it ain't gonna last."

I *do* know. So I'm outta here. I do not intend to miss it.

Chapter Twenty-four

By the Numbers

When I was a kid, I fished by the numbers. Even worm fishing in my local ponds, I counted every stunted sunfish, perch, and horned pout I caught, and I carried a tape so I could put a number on the day's biggest fish. When I went with one of my buddies, I counted his fish as well as my own, and if he was catching more than I was, I fished harder. I didn't like to lose.

I recorded all the numbers in my log. They were the measure of my skill.

As I got older, it gradually changed. I never stopped trying to catch fish, but when I didn't, it was okay. I was satisfied to compete against the fish, or against a particularly challenging fish, or against myself, and getting skunked or outfished didn't bother me.

Keeping score was for kids, and I thought I'd left that behind me.

Then I met Lyle.

Andy and I hired Lyle from a local fly shop to show us his river. When we told him it was the first day of our two-week Montana vacation and that we'd never fished this famous trout river before, he grinned. "You boys're gonna like it," he said. "We'll do a twelve-mile float through the prettiest valley you've ever seen. We got ourselves a beautiful summer day, and we'll see lots of wildlife. I expect the trout'll be rising, too."

It sounded perfect.

We launched Lyle's driftboat a couple of miles downstream from the dam and, at his insistence, tied on No. 14 Royal Wulff dry flies. "These trout ain't real picky," he said. "Just throw 'em out there."

So we drifted and cast our flies, me from the bow and Andy from the stern, and the stresses of day-to-day life back east soon seemed distant and unimportant. With an occasional pull on his oars, Lyle kept us drifting along with the placid currents. We saw deer, moose, and eagles. Wildflowers rioted along the banks, and puffy white clouds dotted the big Montana sky. We took photographs, drank coffee, and told stories. There were plenty of rising trout, and they weren't real picky.

I quickly lost track of time, but I guess we'd been on the river for a couple of hours when Andy netted and released another fat rainbow. "Well," said Lyle, "that puts Andy ahead, five to four."

I turned around. On the boat seat beside Lyle was one of those handheld clickers they use to count traffic at busy intersections. He was actually keeping score. I glanced up at Andy, who rolled his eyes and shrugged, and I knew what he was thinking: We hadn't come here to compete with each other, but Lyle was a nice guy and we didn't want to spoil his fun.

Every hour or so, Lyle announced the score. I figured Andy, like me, was ignoring it. It was Lyle's thing. Some guides like to use numbers to measure their own ability, like kids. Good for business, probably, and a way to know how you stack up against other guides. Counting would keep you from lying, too.

When we beached the boat for lunch, the score was Andy twelve, Bill nine. More than twenty trout in four or five hours. We'd had a terrific morning, and Lyle was whistling and smiling as he laid out the food.

I pulled Andy aside. "Can you believe it?" I said. "This guy's keeping score."

Andy shrugged. "Who cares? Don't worry about it."

"Easy for you to say," I said with a quick smile. "You're winning."

Andy cocked his head and started to say something when Lyle called us for lunch.

Lyle insisted we swap ends for the afternoon float. "To keep things even," he explained. As I took the stern seat, it occurred to me that for the rest of the day Andy, up in the bow, would have the advantage of casting to new water. It didn't seem quite fair. He was already ahead of me. I didn't say anything. But I wondered if I'd be able to catch up with him.

I began to scan the upcoming water more closely. I made longer casts, paid more attention to mending my line, took greater care to hook the fish that took my fly, and fought them gingerly so I could land those that I hooked. I fished with one eye on Andy. If there were eagles soaring overhead or moose munching weeds along the bank, I didn't notice them.

In the middle of the afternoon, Lyle announced, "Bill's pulled into the lead, sixteen to fourteen. Close match, folks. Anybody's ball game."

Then, I noticed, Andy's casts began to zing over the water in long graceful loops, dropping his fly precisely into the paths of rising trout. I counted three trout for Andy while I took none, and I knew, even before Lyle's announcement, that Andy had pulled back into the lead. Andy knew it, too. I could see it in the jut of his chin and the tense hunch of his shoulders.

Somewhere along the way, we'd stopped praising each other's trout and joking about our own flubs. Neither of us took time out to rest our casting wrists or sip a Coke. Whenever Andy hooked a fish, I found myself hoping he'd lose it. When I had one on, Andy just kept casting. We fished grimly, we caught trout, and Lyle announced the score every hour.

Finally, he said, "Less than a mile to takeout and Andy's out in front, twenty-two, nineteen."

I scanned the water, spotted a riser, dropped my Royal Wulff over him, and caught him. When I looked up, I saw a trout sip in Andy's fly. He hesitated too long before lifting his rod, and I heard him mutter, "Nuts!"

I caught another. Andy missed two more strikes. Then he hooked one that, unaccountably, broke off. I missed one, then landed another.

"All tied up," Lyle announced. "This one's going right down to the wire. Takeout's just around the bend."

I hastily dried off my fly, spotted a rise, and cast to it. As the white-winged Wulff drifted toward it, I noticed that Andy had sat down. His line was dragging on the water and he was fiddling with his reel. Just then a trout sucked in my fly. I hauled back as hard as I could. My tippet popped and my line came flying back over my head. "Shoot," I grumbled. I reeled in and sat down.

Lyle veered toward the boat landing. "It's still tied," he said. "We can go for overtime. Sudden death. How about it? I'll drop the anchor right here."

"My reel's busted," said Andy.

"I'm all out of flies," I said.

"Well, too bad," said Lyle. "Kiss your sister, then, boys."

After Lyle dropped us off at our cabin, Andy said, "I never saw you bust off a trout like you did on that last one. And I happen to know you've got a million flies."

"Yeah," I said, "well, a hundred bucks says there's nothing wrong with your reel. And I saw you purposely miss all those fish there at the end."

He chuckled. "Somewhere along the way I realized that I didn't want to win."

"For a while there," I said, "I did. And I didn't like it."

Chapter Twenty-five

Only Yesterday

Yesterday Sarah, my eight-year-old daughter, caught her first trout on a fly rod. It was a wild, silvery little cutthroat, seven or eight inches long, and it flashed up from the pool in front of our campsite, clamped down on the Royal Wulff she'd cast out there, and leapt the instant it felt the hook.

"Got one," she said, as if she'd been catching trout on dry flies all her life. She stripped it in, knelt on the sand beach, unhooked it, and released it without ceremony.

For three days, we'd been rafting the Middle Fork of the Salmon River in Idaho's Frank Church River of No Return Wilderness. Three days without television, telephones and computers, without showers, flushing toilets, and beds or sheets.

Three days of Class III rapids, of mountain goats perched high on canyon walls, of eagles and ospreys, of Dutch-oven cooking, of sleeping bags, tents and portable toilets, of cold nights and hot days and sudden thunderstorms.

Sarah was two thousand miles from her comfortable suburban home, and I'd been a little nervous about this adventure. If she was miserable, well, there was no return. A week on what must be the wildest river in the country. Once you started, you couldn't change your mind. There were no roads in this wilderness. Just a one-way trip down the river between towering canyon walls in our puny little convoy of rubber rafts.

Sarah had not been miserable. On the second day, in the middle of an afternoon downpour, huddled deep in her slicker with rainwater dripping off her nose, she laughed. "Fun, huh?" she said.

For three days she watched me cast off the back of our raft, drifting bushy Wulffs and Humpies along the shadows of the canyon walls and through the pools and riffles. The river was full of those quick, naive, absolutely wild cutts. Sarah had kept count of those I boated, and sometimes I handed her the rod so she could strip them in.

Life as a Metaphor for Fly Fishing

—

And then yesterday, after supper, she picked up my fly rod and walked down to the beach. I followed after her and sat on a rock, back in the shadows, and watched. She slopped around for a while, but if she'd wanted instruction, she'd have asked for it, so I clamped my tongue between my teeth. And pretty soon, she was casting. She got fifteen or twenty feet of line in the air, and she threw it upstream, followed it down with her rod the way she'd seen me do it, lifted, and cast again.

Across the river, the sun painted the top of the rocky canyon wall in gold. Directly overhead, the sky was still blue. But down there in the darkening bottom of the canyon where we were, Sarah was just a slender silhouette with a ponytail.

A couple times she said, "Oh! I had a strike."

I couldn't resist. "You've got to lift your rod," I said. "You've got to be quick like the fish."

"I *know*, Dad," she said with eight-year-old exasperation.

"Sorry, honey."

A few minutes later, she caught that trout and landed it and released it before it occurred to me to run for a camera. Then she reeled in, came back to where I was sitting, and climbed up on the rock beside me. "There," she said. "That wasn't so hard."

"I never said it was hard," I said. "I only said it was fun."

But I was thinking: I wonder if this is the beginning? I wonder if Sarah will become a fly fisherman? Is she hooked?

I was also thinking: It doesn't matter. This may not turn out to be a pivotal event in her life, but it will always be a Moment for me, and I hope my memory of it never dims.

"Oh, sure," said Sarah. "It *was* fun."

* * *

I lied.

It wasn't yesterday. It only seems that way. Sarah's a senior in college now.

In fact, I hadn't thought about her first trout for years. But this morning I randomly took my 1988 fishing journal off the shelf and thumbed through it, and when I came to the notation for August 14, I stopped.

Third day on the Middle Fork. Mountain goats. Nearly capsized. Lots of small cutts on Humpies. Dutch-oven chicken for supper. Sarah's first dry-fly trout, with no help from me.

When I read that, the memory of it, every detail, came washing over me.

Life as a Metaphor for Fly Fishing

—

That's the value of a journal. It keeps the memories alive and vivid. The older I get, the more I cherish the memories—and the more help I need in summoning them up.

I got into the record-keeping habit as a kid. My father kept a log, so I did, too. Back then, my journal was a straightforward record of my angling prowess. I drew columns in a cheap school notebook and recorded the sizes and numbers of the fish I caught, which was all that mattered. I left space in the margin for notes, such as, "Rain," or "Ran out of worms."

Eventually I got bored with counting my fish, so I stopped drawing columns and substituted narrative summaries. Those summaries still emphasized my success—or lack thereof—but I also began to take note of factors that seemed to contribute to the fishing—weather, water conditions, and baits, lures, and flies that worked. Gradually, anecdotes began to slip into my narratives. Some of them had nothing to do with catching fish.

August 23—Secret Spring Creek—A big bull moose stepped into the water directly across from me to eat. He'd stick his head underwater and come up with weeds draped on his antlers. Each time his head went under, I took a few steps closer to him, snapping pictures with my little pocket camera, peering through the lens all the while, which made him look smaller and farther away than he was. When I looked up, Mr. Moose was looming over me, no more than fifteen feet away, and he was glaring down at me. I got the hell out of there.

Somewhere along the way, I realized that an odd thing was happening: I began to think about what I would write in my journal while I was fishing. Keeping a record became part of the fishing experience itself. I found myself paying more attention to details, things I wanted to remember to write down, variables such as wind and water temperature, barometric pressure, time of day and season, fish behavior, insect activity—anything that might prove significant.

I also became more aware of other things—the birds I saw, the wildflowers that bloomed on the riverbanks, the conversations with my partners, the jokes we told, the people we met, the food we ate. "I must remember to write about that," I'd tell myself.

Aug 21—Scarboro Marsh with Keith—He caught a nice striper on his first cast. I said, "What if that were the only fish we caught all day?" We laughed. As it turned out, it was.

I started carrying a pocket notebook with me, and I jotted notes into it, things I didn't want to forget, memory fragments I didn't want to lose. And when I got home, I converted those notes into expanded journal entries. A fishing trip wasn't over until I'd finished writing down my record of it.

Keeping a journal, I'm convinced, helped me learn how to write stories for magazines. It honed my awareness of detail, encouraged me to look for meaning, and shifted my attention away from numbers to more important things.

It made each fishing trip a fuller, richer experience.

Nowadays I keep my journal in my computer. Every New Year's Day, I print out several copies and send them to my companions, so they can share my memories and relive them as I do: as if they happened only yesterday.

Chapter Twenty-six

High Stakes
and Penny-Ante

The neoprene-clad bottom half of my body dangled in the frigid water, and my upper half huddled miserably in my slicker. Raindrops bounced off my hood like birdshot. The wind slapped waves against the side of my float tube, throwing spray into my face.

Andy was suspended in his own tube a hundred feet away, a blurry shape through the slanting rain. He was still casting, of course, driving tight loops through the wind.

He wasn't catching anything, either.

I glanced at my watch. Nearly one. We had been bobbing on this little nameless pond for five hours. The speckled mayflies should have appeared on the water by now, and the big trout should have cruised out from their hiding places in the weeds to eat them.

No bugs. No trout. Just rain and wind.

With luck, in an hour or so I might persuade Andy to quit. My partner doesn't quit easily. But the *Callibaetis* weren't going to hatch. It wasn't going to happen. I found myself hoping it wouldn't. I just wanted a hot mug of coffee, a long steamy shower. I was ready to cash in.

* * *

Back in the summer of '90 Andy and I had tracked a rumor over an eighty-mile dirt road to this tiny Montana pond. And when we paddled out in our tubes, we saw the rainbows cruising in the shallow, weedy, vodka-clear water. They were exactly and without exaggeration what we'd heard they'd be. Monsters. Leviathans. Twenty-six, twenty-eight inches long. They were so big they were scary. The trout of a lifetime, every one of them. "Probably not more'n a hundred or so live there," our source had confided. "But they're all big. They eat the *Callibaetis* when they hatch. With a good imitation and long skinny tippets—and luck—you might be able to catch one."

Life as a Metaphor for Fly Fishing

—

The chance to hook just one of those mammoth rainbows was enough. We quickly learned that they hadn't grown big by eating things that didn't look right. Conventional dry flies, compared to the real mayflies that tippy-toed on the pond's glassy surface, looked—well, they looked like conventional dry flies, and on that day back in 1990, not a single trout confused them with the real thing.

So we got skunked.

After that, I kept dreaming about those cruising trout. One of them had eaten a bug not more than ten feet from where I sat in my tube. He had drifted into my periphery, hovered not more than three inches under the *Callibaetis* dun, cocked an eye at it, then casually poked his nose out of the water and sipped it in. I could distinguish every vermiculation on his back. The pink slash on his side was the color of salmon flesh.

He was as long as my arm. No exaggeration.

Back home, I tied flies to fool that fish. No-Hackles with extended bodies, clever shuck-dragging emergers, flies intended to be perfect imitations of the *Callibaetis* that hatched in that pond. One day we'd return, and with the right fly, on the right day, with the right sort of luck . . .

Pocket Water

—

* * *

There was no sense casting. I had seen no mayflies, no trout. I hugged myself against the windswept rain and watched Andy cast. *Soon*, I figured. Even Andy would quit eventually.

We had come two thousand miles for this. We had rented a motel room and a car and float tubes, given up a week of income—to be miserable and to see no fish.

A brook winds through the woods across the street from my house in Massachusetts. It's heavily stocked and heavily fished, but most anglers avoid the boggy, mosquito-infested meadow section. An old beaver dam forms a pool where I can count on catching a few trout almost anytime. The fish run a uniform nine inches. They are hatchery browns and brookies, and they all look the same—gray on top and fish-belly white underneath.

A holdover brown with buttery flanks and pretty red spots, a solid twelve-incher, lives in a tricky eddy created by an alder sweeper a hundred feet upstream of the pond. I've raised him twice, hooked him once, briefly, but never landed him.

As I rocked in the rain on that desolate Montana pond, I remembered my little stream. I remembered it fondly. Hell, I missed it.

I found myself wishing I were there. It probably wasn't raining back in Massachusetts. My pod of nine-inchers would be rising in the beaver pond, and I'd catch a few in the hour or two before dark. I'd try for that nice brown trout in the tricky eddy, too, and even if I didn't catch anything, I'd lose only a couple of hours— and a couple of hours of trout fishing on a fine June evening was never a loss.

But a whole day in this rain and wind . . .

I laughed aloud. Then I glanced at Andy. He was still casting. He hadn't heard me, which was a good thing. Andy's an eminent psychiatrist as well as an obsessive fly fisherman. I didn't need his analysis of some neurotic fool who would laugh aloud in the freezing rain when the trout weren't rising.

I remembered the countless times I had prowled the meadow across the street casting dry flies to flaccid little hatchery trout— and dreaming of this desolate Montana pond with its alligator trout.

I always seemed to find myself wishing I were somewhere else.

* * *

My grandfather used to play penny-ante poker. He kept his pennies in a Mason jar. The level of pennies in his jar never seemed to rise or fall very much, and I don't believe he ever counted them. When he came home from his Friday-night games, he always announced that he'd broken even.

"You can't get rich playing penny-ante," Grampie used to say. "But it's relaxing and fun, and you can't lose, either."

A lot of fishermen are like that.

I know a few men who *have* gotten rich gambling for high stakes, but most go broke that way. They lose their wives and become alcoholics, which doesn't seem to deter them.

A lot of fishermen are like that, too.

* * *

I love the big quest with its potential for a big payoff. I've stared at saltwater flats from the bow of a skiff for a week, hoping for just a glimpse of a cruising tarpon or permit. I've made a thousand casts into an Atlantic salmon river and never moved a fish, and then cast another thousand times.

Usually, in high-stakes games, you lose big. You get rained on, and you get skunked. But the chance for an arm-long trout keeps you coming back.

I like the penny-ante times, too—a soft summer afternoon when the dragonflies dart over lily pads and frogs grump in the shallows and bluegills gobble my poppers, or a few hours on a

Life as a Metaphor for Fly Fishing

—

223

June evening with just a spool of tippet and one box of flies in my shirt pocket, wet wading, and naive hatchery trout eating whatever's on the end of my leader.

The problem, of course, is that bluegills conjure up dreams of two-foot trout, while a desolate rain-swept Montana pond makes me yearn for the brook across the street.

* * *

Eventually Andy reeled in and paddled over.

"Had enough?" I said.

"Never. But enough for today."

"I was actually wishing we were back home catching blue-gills," I said.

"That's what you were laughing about, huh?"

I nodded.

He shrugged. "No pain, no gain."

"Sometimes there's a lot of pain with no gain whatsoever."

"There's always gain," said Andy.

Chapter Twenty-seven

The Sweet Spot

June in the Catskills. A couple of weeks shy of the longest day of the year. I had set my alarm for half an hour before sunrise, but I didn't need it. I had drifted off to sleep reviewing my memories of the Bridge Pool, and I had slept fitfully and dreamfully, and I was wide awake before the alarm went off.

My dream featured a trout even larger than the actual trout I'd failed to catch from the Bridge Pool the previous June. That actual trout had been eighteen or nineteen inches long. Maybe twenty. He'd been sipping sunrise spinners against the far bank in the shadowy eddy where a square boulder jutted into the current. I had spotted the little blip of his riseform—about the same disturbance a blueberry would make if you dropped it into the water from a height of one foot—and then spent half an hour figuring out where to stand and how much slack to throw into the longish reach cast that was needed to drift a fly over him without drag. Once I'd found my position—about a forty-five-degree angle upstream and across from him—I was able to spot the fish's ghosty form each time he edged away from the boulder's shadow to eat, and I measured his feeding rhythm. He was unquestionably the biggest trout I'd ever encountered on this famous trout stream.

It had taken another fifteen or twenty minutes of trial and error to figure out what he was eating from the smorgasbord of spinners and spent caddisflies that drifted on the water. The trout told me when he lifted his nose and my No. 20 rusty hen-wing spinner with a peacock-herl thorax drifted into his open mouth.

I hadn't expected it, of course. So my reflexes instead of my brain reacted, and I lifted my rod too quickly and plucked the fly cleanly out of his mouth.

The trout in my dream porpoised out of the water each time he ate, an arrogant head-and-shoulders rise intended to taunt me by flaunting his full length and fatness. When he rose, his eye stared directly into mine. This dream trout was at least thirty inches long. It didn't matter, because in my dream every cast fell in limp coils around my knees. He kept rising, that big eye staring at me with what might have been pity, or contempt, while I flailed around, and I could not get a cast beyond the tip of my absurd twig of a rod.

* * *

The stars were beginning to wink out and the sky over the Catskills was just fading from purple to pewter when I slipped out of the motel and into my car. The whole question was: Would I be the first angler at the Bridge Pool? On this weekend in June, the town swarmed with automobiles displaying Trout Unlimited decals on the back windows and wearing more license plates from Pennsylvania, Massachusetts, and Connecticut than from New York. I actually spotted one from Michigan and another from West Virginia.

I knew exactly where I wanted to be standing. I had a rendezvous with a trout. If not that specific big trout that had lived in the eddy behind the boulder last year, then another big trout that had settled in the same place. There's a sweet spot in every pool, and the biggest resident trout always occupies it. I'd found that sweet spot in the Bridge Pool, which was the sweetest pool on the river.

Pocket Water

—

The New York DEC had cleared a parking area overlooking the Bridge Pool, and they'd built a wooden platform over the water for handicapped anglers. The pool was no secret. Even without the amenities, you couldn't miss it. At its head it emerged from the evergreen forest, tumbled around boulders, flowed under the bridge, then widened and deepened and slowed. It was classic.

But that sweet spot where the big trout lived—I had discovered that all by myself.

I clenched my fist and muttered "Yes!" when I found the lot empty of vehicles. I'd done it. I'd beaten the crowd.

I didn't linger in the car to admire the way mist was wafting off the water or to marvel at the fingers of pink that were clawing into the sky. I leapt out, tugged on my waders, strung my rod, and waded in.

It had been a year, but the memory of it remained vivid, and I found the exact place where I had stood. I tied on a No. 20 rusty spinner with a peacock-herl thorax and fingered some Gink into it—not because I believed my trout would necessarily be eating rusty spinners this morning, but for luck, and for tradition, and for lack of a better idea.

Life as a Metaphor for Fly Fishing

—

A few smallish trout splashed and spurted in front of me, but I ignored them. I focused on the shadowy eddy behind the square boulder.

The first time he rose, I thought it was my imagination, wishful thinking. The image had burned so deeply into my mind a year earlier that it had sometimes appeared when I was staring out my office window at the snow on my lawn, or driving a highway, or falling asleep at night.

No, he *was* there, and when I squinted through my polarized glasses, I saw the shape of him. He could have been the same trout, grown an inch or two longer in the year since I'd yanked my fly out of his mouth.

I resisted the urge to begin casting immediately. I let him come up several times to whet his appetite and gain courage, while I gauged his rhythm.

My first cast fell short, and I slid it away before it could drag over him. On my next cast, he stuck up his nose and ate before my fly got to him.

My third cast was on the water, neatly air-mended, perfectly timed, and I knew this was the one. I reminded myself not to strike too soon when he ate my fly, to let him close his mouth and turn his head so the hook would catch in the corner of his mouth when I lifted my rod and tightened on him . . .

That's when a length of bright yellow fly line came floating past me. When I looked up, I saw that the line was attached to a rod, and the rod was being held by a fisherman. He had waded into the Bridge Pool while I was focused on my trout, and he was now standing barely ten feet upstream from where I stood, casting across and down, covering the water directly in front of me.

My first—irrational—thought was that I was still deep in my fishing-frustration dream, that I was back in my motel room waiting for the alarm clock to wake me up.

My second thought was that if I had a gun . . .

"Hello?" I said to the guy. "Excuse me?"

"Hi, there," he said pleasantly. "Beautiful morning, eh?" He looked to be in his early thirties. He was wearing a cowboy hat and a pair of those new breathable waders and a vest festooned with gadgets and geegaws. I couldn't tell what kind of rod he was using, but it was a nice one, and I recognized the reel. It was a very expensive reel. It looked brand new.

"Am I invisible?" I said.

He frowned. "Huh?"

"I mean, can you see me?"

He smiled. "Oh, sure. Plain as day."

"Just checking," I said. "Am I in your way?"

"Oh, no," he said. "Don't worry about it. You're fine."

I took a deep breath. "Look," I said. "There's a nice fish right in front of me."

"What?" he said. "Where?" He ripped his line off the water in front of me, made a couple of false casts, and splashed it down beside the rock where my trout had been rising. "There?"

* * *

So I reeled in, waded out of the Bridge Pool, sat on the handicapped casting ramp, and watched that guy cast at my fish.

I couldn't decide whether to be amused or furious—at his astounding lack of courtesy, at his apparent immunity to sarcasm, at the ironic predictive truth of my fishing dream.

I remembered the time some guy had come sloshing downstream to cast over a rising trout my partner was casting upstream to and how they'd ended up standing toe to toe debating ownership of that fish. I remembered all the times I'd nearly been run down by driftboats while wading. This wasn't the first time I'd been shouldered out of a pool I thought I had to myself.

The guy kept casting at my trout. He wasn't very skilled, and I was delighted that he didn't catch it.

I pondered easy generalizations—how Hollywood has made fly fishing too damn popular, how the schools, shows, books, and videos do a great job of teaching fly casting, entomology, and knots but a lousy job of teaching manners, how contemporary society rewards competitiveness, aggressiveness, and selfishness and punishes old-fashioned civility.

I'd set my alarm so I could get here first and stake my righteous claim to the sweetest spot on the entire river.

And I'd succeeded. I'd beaten everybody. I'd won, dammit.

That was my spot, my fish.

Wasn't it?

Chapter Twenty-eight

The Compleatly Neurotic Angler

I'll admit I was a bit nervous about seeing a shrink. But Dr. Izaak's office building put me at ease. It was a log cabin tucked into a grove of pines at the end of a long dirt road. An English setter lay on his side in the dusty path that led up to the porch, and I could hear the gurgle of a river from beyond the pines out back. The screened porch reminded me of my own: A pair of patched waders sprawled beside the door, and a battered old bamboo fly rod hung on pegs. A bedraggled Muddler was hooked in the keeper ring. Good all-around choice. It inspired confidence.

"You're crazy," Charlie had told me the previous Sunday afternoon when I threw my new Loomis 4-weight into the Church

Pool of the Farmington River. "They're eating caddis pupae, not graphite."

I went over my waders retrieving the rod, and in the car on the way home, I said to Charlie, "You were right about what you said when I threw my rod."

"Naw. I was wrong. They were on little sulphur emergers."

"I mean about me being crazy."

Charlie nodded. "Maybe you should see Doc Izaak," he said. "Sanest fisherman I know. He helped me."

"A shrink?"

Charlie nodded.

"What was your problem?"

"Piscoschizophrenia."

I tried to pronounce it and failed. "What's that?"

"I identified with fish in an unnatural way. Especially brown trout." He handed me a business card. It read: "Walter Izaak, psychotherapy. Specialist in angling neuroses."

* * *

I banged on the screen door. From inside came a man's voice. "Hang on. I'm in the middle of a whip-finish."

I didn't like the sound of that, but I waited, and a couple of minutes later the door opened. Specks of grizzly hackle, gray dubbing, and silver tinsel were tangled in the doctor's beard, and a colorful bauble hung from his right earlobe. I wasn't sure how I felt about a shrink who wore an earring.

"I'm Charlie's friend," I said. "I got an appointment."

"Oh, right," said Izaak. "Charlie still like brown trout?"

"Very much. Very, *very* much."

He shrugged. "Charlie's a sick man." He opened the door for me. "Well, come in, come in. I ain't got all day, you know."

As I entered, I got a better look at his earring. It was a fish-hook, about a No. 8, turned-up eye. A Tiemco 7999, if I wasn't mistaken. One jungle cock nail, some lime-colored floss, and a few golden-pheasant fibers clung to it.

"Have a seat." He gestured at a camp stool in the corner. "Tell me about it."

"There's so many things, I hardly know where to start."

"Relax, son. Think of your favorite trout river. Let it flow."

I leaned back against the wall and let my eyes close. Through the cabin's open windows I could hear the rush and tinkle of the stream out back and the hiss of the breeze sifting through the pines. The cabin smelled of mothballs and wet dog. It was comforting. "For example," I began, "the day Charlie suggested I see you? I threw my rod into the river and then filled my waders getting it back."

"Rod throwing is seriously disturbed behavior," Izaak said. "I don't usually associate with people who throw rods."

"I don't blame you. But that's not it. It's wading in too deep. Every time I go fishing I fill my waders. There always seems to be a trout rising just beyond my range, so I inch my way out there, and before I know it the river's trickling in under my armpits. Once I got caught in the middle of the Deerfield when they released water from the dam. Another time I hooked this monster rainbow in the Box Canyon—"

"Depth Wish," he said.

"Huh?"

"You got a Depth Wish, son. Eros and thanatos. Freud tells us that we're all born with a Depth Wish. Perfectly normal. Feel better?"

"Not exactly," I said. "Anyway, that's not all. That new Loomis? The one I chucked into the Church Pool? See, it's not that I needed that rod. I got about six dozen rods. Thing is, every time I run into another fisherman, I admire his rod. Can't seem to keep my eyes off other guys' rods. And no matter what they're using, I want one just like it. Guy waving around some old fiberglass stick? I gotta have an old fiberglass stick just like his."

"What about bass boats with long pointy noses and big out-board motors, stuff like that?"

"Just rods," I said. "I got a thing for fishing rods."

Dr. Izaak nodded. "Sounds like Rod Envy."

"Is Rod Envy serious?" I said.

"It's a stage," he said. "Everybody, one time or another, they see some guy's rod, they feel a little inadequate, wish they had a better rod. Went through that myself. You just gotta try to enjoy your own rod, be satisfied with what you got." He glanced at his watch. "So, if that's it . . ."

I sighed. "There's more. See, the reason I threw my rod that time was that I couldn't figure out what fly to tie on. Happens all the time. Tie on a little cut-wing olive, one cast, and I think I oughta be using maybe a Comparadun or a No-Hackle. So I go digging back into my fly box. Spend more time tying knots than I do casting."

"Can't keep your fingers out of your fly box, huh?"

"Exactly."

"You got a Fly Fetish, I'm afraid."

"That sounds bad."

"Bad?" He rolled his eyes. "Look," he said finally, "I'm going to suggest a new approach, sort of an aversion therapy for this

Fly Fetish of yours. It's still experimental, and it could backfire. You game?"

"Anything," I said. "I'm desperate."

"The idea was developed out west. They hold this contest. The One-Fly tournament? The idea is, before you start out, you pick one fly. That's the one you use all day. Bust it off, you're done. Maybe you lie awake all night wondering what to use, but your important time, the fishing time, you have to devote to fishing, because right or wrong, you're stuck with that fly."

I felt beads of sweat pop out on my forehead. "Suppose I just cut back on the number of fly boxes I carry in my vest . . ."

"Cold turkey," he said. "It's the only way, son. Now—"

"There's something else."

He sighed.

"It's nymphs," I said. "I got a thing for nymphs. I love looking at them, I love tying them, and I love fishing with them. Even now, just mentioning it to you, I can feel my pulse racing. There are times when I feel like if I don't go do a little nymphing I'll go nuts. Nymphs are kind of a passion with me, you might say. My wife blew her stack the other night. Said I woke her up mumbling 'Pheasant Tail' in my sleep. I tried to explain, but she thought I said 'pleasant.'"

The doctor cleared his throat. "Self-control," he said. "About the only thing you can do for Nymph-O-Mania if you don't wanna get in serious trouble. We done yet?"

"One more thing," I said. "See, normally I'm a pretty good fly caster. I practice all the stuff Mrs. Wulff writes about. I'm proud of my casting ability. But at certain times it all deserts me. I whack the water behind me, snag a tree, hook myself in the ear—"

"I used to do that," he said, fingering his earlobe.

"For example," I continued, "Charlie and I were fishing the Deerfield last week. It was getting dark and I was trying to get a drift over a nice fish sipping spinners in a little eddy. Charlie says it's time to go. I tell him hang on a minute. So he gives me five casts. That did it. Very next cast I hung the tree behind me."

"This happens whenever your casts are rationed out?"

"Exactly. We're in a canoe, Charlie says it's his turn in the bow, gives me just two more casts? Guaranteed I'll mess 'em both up. Ration my casts and it's disaster."

"All fishermen go through the same thing," said Izaak. "The Cast Ration Complex. You'll outgrow it." He cleared his throat. "So. We done?"

I sighed. "Yes. I guess that's it."

"Good. Because I've got a date with a rainbow trout." He sighed. "She's gorgeous—beautiful rosy complexion, perfect body, big but perfectly proportioned. Sleek. You ought to see her pectorals, the curve of her tail . . ."

"You gonna try that Muddler?" I said.

"Don't be crazy," said Izaak. "I'm gonna go dig some worms."